The Death of a Man

The Key to "Life"

"I am crucified with Christ, nevertheless I live."
Galatians 2:20

by

Ted Tenney

© Copyright, 2014
By
Ted Tenney

ISBN: 978-1-935802-13-6

All rights reserved. No part of this publication may be reproduced, stored in a retrieval system, or transmitted in any form or by any means, electronic, mechanical, photocopying, recording, or otherwise, without the prior written permission of the publisher.

Cover art by Honey Hilliard

FATHER
&
SON
PUBLISHING, INC.
4909 N. Monroe Street
Tallahassee, Florida 32303-7015
www.fatherson.com
800-741-2712

Preface

When I was a child growing up in church, I was always disturbed when I heard the phrase, "die to self." I was worried that somehow I should not be the "me" I knew myself to be. I, like many others, was confused about the meaning of this phrase. I thought that this meant that I couldn't have any fun in life that would bring pleasure to my "self." I would later come to realize that if I died to my current life of self-centeredness, then God would give me a new life of righteousness, joy, and peace. I learned that's something to look forward to and embrace, not fear! The Apostle Paul made it clear in his letter written to the churches in the region of Galatia.

> *I have been crucified with Christ and I no longer live, but Christ lives in me. The life I live in the body, I live by faith in the Son of God, who loved me and gave Himself for me"*
> *(Gal. 2:20).*

Knowing that Jesus loves me and died for me illuminates my mind and my spirit to life's realities and fulfills my deepest longings. It gives me a sense of purpose, but it solicits a definitive response. It is by faith that we accept Christ into our hearts and lives as Lord and Savior, allowing Him to live His life and His will through us. The decision to die to self puts us on a journey, a new path of hope which leads to eternal peace in our eternal relationship with God. This book is about that journey. I trust you will enjoy the book and enjoy the journey!

Introduction

The death of a man is the key to life. It is the only means to a happy, abundant and eternal life. Jesus, God's son, is the key. There is no where else to turn.

"Simon Peter answered Him, Lord, to whom shall we go? You have the words of eternal life" (John 6:68).

"You are the Christ, the Son of the living God," proclaimed Peter. In spite of the confusion and doubt that prevailed in the society around him, the great Apostle Peter recognized Jesus for who He really was (and is). Jesus affirmed Peter, remarking that only God could have opened his eyes to that revelation. Then Jesus added that upon the confession of this revelation the "Church" would be built (Matt. 16:16-18). Thus, those today, who believe and confess this same statement of Peter (in spite of the confusion and doubt of their present society), make up the indestructible Church of Jesus Christ. God can, and wants to, open *your* eyes to that same revelation. If you believe that Jesus is God's Son, then you believe that it was God's perfect redemptive plan to send Him to earth to die on the cross as *the* sacrifice for your sins and the sins of the whole world. God's love for His creation, including you and I, was so great that He was willing to give up His Son for us.

> *"For God so loved the world, that He gave His one and only Son, that whoever believes in Him shall not perish but have eternal life (John 3:16).*

Death of a Man

Jesus paid the price for our sins. So now, only through His shed blood can our sins be washed away and forgiven. This plan of "Salvation" is consummated when we believe in the atoning work of Jesus as the substitute for the judgment of our sin and we confess Him as our personal Savior and Lord.

> *"If you confess with your mouth, Jesus is Lord, and believe in your heart that God raised Him from the dead, you will be saved. For it is with your heart that you believe and are justified, and it is with your mouth that you confess and are saved"* **(Rom. 10: 9, 10).**

When we do this, God not only faithfully forgives us of our sins, but He also promises us eternal life in Heaven. This book is about the death of "that" man, Jesus. But it is also about the death of "a" man, any man, or woman, all of mankind.

The *Death of a Man* is not a new philosophy, not a new religion, or even a unique viewpoint. It is a way of life taught by God in His Word, for anyone who longs to be a "Christian." A Christian is a child of the living God, a disciple of Jesus, the Son of God. This book is designed to walk through the steps of the last few days of Jesus' life in order to know how to follow Him and be like Him.

Some choose to believe on Jesus and invite Him into their lives to help them live peacefully and happy all their days upon the earth. Others are content to ask God for help, whenever they feel they need it, as they attempt to live righteously as a Christian. However, some are not content to live a mediocre Christian life just trying to be "happy" or "religious." Some have a deep desire to know God personally and intimately and to be as much like His Son, Jesus, as they possibly can each and every day.

Death of a Man

I have used a lot of scripture in this book. The fact is that this book is a message from God simply packaged in a different form or arrangement. This message has been burning inside of me for over 30 years. You will find the pronouns you and we are interchangeable throughout this text. The fact is that we are all in this together. None of us have made it yet. We are on this journey each and every day.

This book is designed for individual or small group study with thought-provoking questions at the end of each chapter. As children of God, we are called to follow in the steps of Jesus. He is our example. The word "Christian" literally means, "little christs." That is why it's recorded in three of the four gospels, Jesus' words, "Take up your cross and follow me." We must say like the apostle Paul, "I am crucified with Christ" (Gal. 2:20). We too must die, but how? Let me take you on a journey from the garden to the grave, and beyond. Those who truly experience "The Death of a Man" will find true happiness, contentment, and a life that is abundant and eternal. The "Life" that God, Himself, has promised. Let's begin the journey of a lifetime.

Contents

Chapter 1	The Garden	1
Chapter 2	The Valley	13
Chapter 3	The Judgement	25
Chapter 4	The Road	39
Chapter 5	The Cross	49
Chapter 6	The Death	61
Chapter 7	The Resurrection	73
Chapter 8	The Spirit	83
Chapter 9	The Ascension	99
Chapter 10	The Life	113
Chapter 11	Conclusion	127

1
The Garden

It all started in the garden. It was a beautiful garden, one that would take your breath away at a mere glance. It had a magnificent display of flowers, plants, and trees, all in full bloom. Delicious-looking fruits and vegetables hung from every branch and vine. Apples, oranges, and bananas were all perfectly ripened. A freshness of life simply permeated this place of paradise. Into this spectacular array of splendor, man was placed by God, His Creator. Man was designed and created to eternally exist in this peaceful environment of pleasure. He was given this beautiful garden to enjoy and care for as he saw fit. In the Garden of Eden, animals freely roamed about to serve as aides in the maintenance of the garden as well as companionship for Adam himself. Adam was given much responsibility in this garden, but none greater than the responsibility of his own will. It was with that will that he would choose between one task or another, one name or another, and one fruit or another. It was with that will that he would choose between good and evil, right and wrong, and obedience or disobedience. Where there is responsibility, there is always consequences. Sometimes you can experience benefits and rewards, while other times it can prove costly.

    God had created woman out of one of Adam's ribs while he slept. When he saw her, he was pleased to have someone that would be perfectly suited to meet his need for love and companionship. He called her Eve. I wish I could say that they fell in love and lived happily ever after. Even though that was the ideal, it didn't quite work out that way. The problem was that Adam and Eve were not the first ones on earth. They found that someone else had already been there, the devil. The once beautiful and powerful angel, Satan, had been thrown out of heaven because of his pride and rebellion against God and he landed on earth along with a legion of other rebellious angels, known today as demons. Since that day until now their objective, under Satan's directives is to counteract all the good that God endeavors to do in and through mankind. It didn't take long for the devil to find an opportunity to deceive Adam and Eve. God had told Adam and Eve that they could eat of any fruit in the garden except for the Tree of Knowledge in the middle of the garden. If they ate of that tree then they would die. However, Satan has a way of twisting things around. He would appeal to their human desires (our weakness). He would tempt them in the three areas where we all are vulnerable to sin and disobey God; the lust of the eyes, the lust of the flesh, and the pride of life. Satan, appearing in the form of a serpent tempted Eve to eat of the forbidden fruit by getting her to focus on the appearance of the fruit, its ability to satisfy her taste buds, and its power to make her wise. That's the model of most temptations; it looks good, it will make me feel good, and it will make me better off. When the temptation becomes stronger than

The Garden

our commitment to be obedient to God's command, then we sin. Satan, the Devil, is a liar and the father of lies (John 8:44). He wants to blind and deceive anyone who might believe in God.

> ***"The god of this age has blinded the minds of unbelievers, so that they cannot see the light of the gospel of the glory of Christ, who is the image of God" (II Cor. 4:4).***

We must beware of his devices and his lies. Adam and Eve fell prey to his deception because they were not grounded in the truth. After the Devil's temptation and Eve's encouragement, Adam also partook of the forbidden fruit. Partaking from that tree opened their eyes to "Good and Evil." However, Adam's decisions not only cost him his right to live in the garden, it cost him his life. His eternal garden existence was cut off. His days were now numbered, along with every man that would ever come after him. He had yielded the right of his own will to an outside influence. The old serpent, the Devil, got Adam to share that right by appealing to his pride and the love of a woman. (What worked back then, is still working today!) This evil influence produced, in Adam, a sinful nature. Not only would he have to contend with that nature his entire life, but he would pass that same nature on to every generation after him.

> ***"Through one man (Adam), sin entered into the world" (Rom. 5:12).***

His paradise turned into a prison. His bondage was now to the earth itself to cultivate it by the sweat of his brow (Gen: 3:19). Adam and Eve would be banished from the garden to never return again. The Garden, which hasn't been seen since, served its intended purpose. It was a place of decision. It was to be a decision of great magnitude, a truly life and death decision.

There was another garden, one not known so much for its fruit. However, it was also a place of decision. Again, it was a matter of life and death. The decision was not whether or not to eat of a tree, but whether or not to hang on one. Adam's choice brought about death for all men, while Jesus' choice meant life for all.

> *"Just as the result of one trespass was condemnation for all men, so also the result of one act of righteousness was justification that brings life for all men" (Rom. 5:18).*

Adam in essence said, not your will, but my will be done. In the Garden of Gethsemane, Jesus prayed to God, the Father just the opposite, for the Father's will to be done, not His own. Adam was only human. He probably thought he was doing the right thing at the time. But he was not taking into account the words and the will of God. (Sound familiar?) Jesus, being the Son of God, was able to draw strength from the relationship that He had with His Father. Jesus had brought His disciples to one of His favorite spots to pray, the Garden of Gethsemane. Knowing what was about to happen, Jesus prayed to God for strength. Unaware of the magnitude of that night, the disciples kept falling asleep while praying. When we realize the lateness of the hour, we will make prayer a priority. Despite the lack of support from His closest friends, Jesus prayed even more earnestly. During such agony of the moment, Jesus literally sweat drops of blood (Luke 22:44). Yet, He was able to make the decision that would please God, in spite of what it would cost Him. It all started in the garden. It was the beginning of the end of which would become a beginning that would never end.

The Garden

The same can be said of you because there is a third garden to consider. It is a garden that man cannot see. This garden is also a place of decision, a matter of life and death. However, unlike the literal gardens of Gethsemane and Eden, this one is a figurative one. It is the garden of your heart. This garden is more beautiful than any other. Within the garden of the heart lies the beauty of love, feelings, and emotions. Therein lies the wonder of imagination and creativity as well as the ability to discern between two choices. Therein also lies the God-given privilege of "Free Will" (the right to choose). Within this garden are a variety of seeds. There are seeds from heredity, environment, experience, and knowledge. You are responsible to cultivate the garden of your heart. Some seeds are good and some are bad. God plants seeds of knowledge and truth into our hearts through a variety of sources. However, the Devil is also planting seeds of deceit and discouragement. Thoughts, images, temptations, and even words are all seeds planted in the soil of our hearts. Many seeds come from other people in the words they say or the things they do. But many times they can come from the music that we listen to or the images we see on television or the internet and what we read. The Devil will try to bombard us with all kinds of seeds to gain a foothold in our hearts.

> ***"Be self-controlled and alert. Your enemy, the Devil prowls around like a roaring lion looking for someone to devour" (I Peter 5:8).***

He knows that he can defeat us spiritually if he can get those bad seeds to take root in our hearts. We have to guard our hearts from evil influences, evil thoughts, and inappropriate images that can easily enter our minds. Especially in this wicked and perverse generation, we need to be alert and act quickly and decisively. The longer you dwell on them, think about them, and nurture them, the more they will grow. The seed enters through the mind and travels to the heart. That journey could only take a few seconds. Knowing this, I like to live by the 7-second rule. Considering that a thought or temptation can easily become a sin of lust or disobedience in as little as a few seconds, I start to immediately count off 7 seconds in my mind. If I linger upon a thought, image, or temptation that is not pleasing to God then I am yielding my heart and spirit to that evil influence. However, as I begin to count, the thought will usually disappear in less than 3 seconds because I have determined, once I start to count, that I am going to deal with this negative thought. I use the number 7 because it's God's perfect number, but as soon as I decide to turn my thoughts to pleasing God, that thought replaces the previous one. The desire to serve and please God overcomes the desire to please self or my flesh. It takes the power of God's Spirit inside of you to overcome any temptation. It only takes a few seconds as you allow His Spirit to have His way. I challenge you to try the 7-second rule yourself, it works! It would always be good to quote any scripture that you know. That is what Jesus did when the Devil tempted Him as recorded in Matthew, chapter 4. The Word of God is powerful. It is truth. It is our weapon against the lies and temptations of the Devil. Often times we can't control the seeds that are tossed in the direction of our hearts. They may even land in a sensitive or fertile place in our heart. However, they will not grow unless they are nurtured and cultivated. That process is in your control. You decide what you will dwell on and act upon. You exercise that "free will" that God has given you to make your own choices. The enemy of our souls will not only drop those seeds of temptation, but he will also sprinkle it with water, like fuel on the fire, in order to

The Garden

stimulate its growth. He loves to sprinkle it with self-justification, trying to make us believe that it's not really that bad. "I'm only human," is a statement contrived for your deception. He loves to sprinkle it with rationalization. Rationalization is the Devil's means to lead us into self-deception. That's when we begin to lie to ourselves. The whole area of defensiveness is a tool that the Devil loves to use and many people fall victim to it. "Everybody's doing it," is another one of his ploys to get that seed to germinate. "I'm not as bad as so and so," leads us down the road to pride and arrogance. I could go on, but I think you get my point. As soon as that seed hits the soil of our heart, it must be destroyed or ignored immediately, before the Devil has time to use it for our demise. The Devil has a bag of seeds labeled, "rebellion." That's his nature and he will do everything in his power to plant those seeds in the soil of your heart in an attempt to get at least one of them to sprout and grow. When they start to grow, they spread uncontrollably, like ivy. You can't stop it, but you can kill it. Don't let it take root, but rather, let the seed of the Word of God grow in you. The seeds that Jesus has to offer us will grow into eternal life. Jesus used the analogy of water instead of seeds when referring to God's Word taking root in one's heart.

> *"But whoever drinks the water I give him will never thirst. Indeed, the water that I give him will become in him a spring of water welling up to eternal life" (John 4:14).*

Seeds, whether they be thoughts or feelings, come from everything and everyone that we come in contact with. But, we have the power to cultivate which ever seeds we choose.

You decide what grows and what dies. You decide to feed the sinful nature that you received from Adam (that gives you momentary pleasure), or you can feed the spiritual nature that you received from God, that gives God pleasure and produces lasting joy in us. Adam's choice brought about death, while Jesus' choice brought life. The decision in the garden of your heart is yours and yours alone. Follow the example of Adam, or follow Jesus! Hear Jesus' words.

> *"If any man would come after me, (be a follower of Mine) he must deny himself and take up his cross and follow Me" (Matt. 16:24).*

Jesus used a word that meant this is something that we must do. It is not a suggestion; it is a requirement, a commandment! But, it all starts with a decision. Have you decided to follow Jesus? It starts in the garden of your heart. If you believe in Jesus, the Son of God, as your personal Savior and Lord, then you will want to follow Him. You must follow Him to the Garden of Gethsemane. However, we must not be like the disciples who fell asleep while praying. Jesus went further than the disciples with His prayer:

> *"Jesus went out as usual to the Mount of Olives, and His disciples followed Him. On reaching the place, He said to them, 'pray that you will not fall into temptation.' He withdrew about a stone's throw beyond them, knelt down and prayed, 'Father, if you are willing, take this cup from me; yet not my will, but yours be done" (Luke 22:39-42).*

Even though the "cup" that Jesus was being asked to take meant His death on the cross, Jesus was still willing. Jesus had told the disciples that they would also drink this same cup

The Garden

(Matt. 20:23), but the disciples weren't ready quite yet. Peter was still operating in his fleshly nature when he, a few minutes later, pulled out his sword to defend his Lord and chopped off the ear of a servant of the High Priest. Jesus rebuked Peter.

> ***"Jesus commanded Peter, 'Put your sword away! Shall I not drink the cup the Father has given me?" (John 18:11).***

Obviously the disciples weren't ready to give up everything for their Master as they all scattered. Jesus was taken away by the chief priests and soldiers. He was all alone; none of His disciples accompanied Him. However, the disciples would later on find the strength to commit fully to the Lord. Following Jesus means staying with Him all the way and not turning back when things look difficult. We must pray with Jesus, "not my will," and take the cup He has given us knowing the price that we will have to pay. He is calling you today to come and follow Him. Will you take this first step in the long journey of following Jesus? If so, read on.

The Garden

Summary Points

- We have the same choice that Adam and Eve had. We can listen to the lies of the Devil and give in to our fleshly desires, or we can obey the commands of God.

- We have the same choice as the disciples had. We can unite in prayer with Jesus realizing the urgency of the hour, or we can be found asleep on our watch.

- When temptation becomes stronger than our commitment to be obedient to God's command, then we sin.

- We decide what thoughts and truths that we will cultivate in our own hearts and lives.

- Where there is responsibility, there is always consequences. There are consequences for all our thoughts and decisions; some are a matter of life and death.

- We have the same choice that Jesus had. We can say, "Not your will, but mine be done, or not my will, but yours be done." The first step is to decide to follow Jesus.

Death of a Man

Personal Reflections

(Also read John 3: 1-21)

1. Do you believe in Jesus? Are you ready to follow Him and say, "not my will's will be done?"

2. What kind of soil do you have in the garden of your heart? (Is it ripe for the things of this world or the things of God?)

3. What seeds are being planted in your heart right now? (What influences are being poured into your heart?)

4. What are the seeds that might be growing in the garden of your heart, which are not pleasing to God?

5. How can you cultivate the seeds of God that have been planted in your heart?

6. In what area of weakness is the Devil trying to trip you up? Are you aware of his lies and deception?

2

The Valley

Just as Jesus finished His life-altering prayer in the garden of Gethsemane, a mob of soldiers and officials of the chief priests and Pharisees came to arrest Jesus. Judas, one of the twelve disciples who had followed Jesus for the previous three years, had been tempted by Satan himself to betray Jesus into the hands of the religious leaders. He later regretted this act, that paid him a mere thirty pieces of silver, and he went out and hung himself (Matt. 27:3-5).

As they led Jesus out of the Garden at the foot of the Mount of Olives they had to cross the Kidron Valley on their way to Jerusalem. The Kidron Valley separated the Mount of Olives and the Temple Mount. The Kidron Valley was known to some as a valley of death. Many kings and prominent leaders were buried there. Today, it is still full of tombs and graves. During the reign of Asa, King of Israel the valley was used to bury the articles of idol worship which had been brought into the Temple of God. God had dealt with the King about the disobedience and idolatry of God's people, the Israelites. They knew that they needed to repent and destroy the ungodly things that had crept into the Temple and into their lives. So they brought all the things that were dishonoring to God, used in their pagan worship of false gods, along with their idols into the valley to be destroyed, burned, and buried. Once they had done that, they were free from their spiritual bondage to idolatry and eligible to receive God's blessings in their lives. Many other kings used this valley for the same purpose. It became a "junk yard" for false idols and the impure things of pagan worship that God strongly disapproved of.

And now, as Jesus walked through the valley, He knew that there were certain things in His life that would have to be destroyed and die there as well. His life was free from idolatry and or disobedience, but yet He was still human. He would have to allow His sense of self-preservation to die in that valley. When He would be accused, He would not retaliate or defend Himself in order to save His life. When He faced death by crucifixion, He did not resist or fight back. He willingly laid his life down. He would have to let go of His rights to be treated fairly or even humanly. He would be abused, beaten, and lied about, yet He said nothing. He had to let go of His feelings of responsibility to provide for His family; His mother and siblings. He knew that He would have to leave them and that they would no longer benefit from His physical, emotional, financial, and or spiritual support. His plan was to leave His mother in the competent hands of His closest friend and follower, John. He would have to let them all go and let His emotional ties to them die. It must have been a grueling and lonely walk through this Kidron Valley as even His closest friends had deserted Him. But He had to let them go too. Those relationships would only hold Him back from what God, the Father, had planned for Him to do. Stripped of His dignity, His rights, His family and friends, Jesus walked through the valley.

The Valley

Gone were His human desires, His comforts, and any thoughts for the comforts and pleasures of this life. Jesus emptied Himself of self until there was nothing left but a spirit willing to do the will of God.

Many Christians today are walking through this same valley, spiritually, being challenged and convicted to rid themselves of the things that would hinder them from doing the will of God in their lives. In order to follow Jesus we must walk through the valley. We must free ourselves from our idol worship, dishonoring habits, fear of loss, entitlements, and relationships that are not pleasing unto the Lord. We can't get to the mountain without going through the valley. It is painful. It takes commitment. It takes sacrifice. We must destroy, burn, and bury the things in our lives that have us in bondage to sin and that are keeping us from receiving from God His intended blessings. Many Christians today don't even realize the spiritual bondage that they are in. The devil has deceived us and just like he did to Eve, he has fed us a pack of lies. We think we deserve this or that. We want our share, to get what's coming to us. The fact is that what we deserve is punishment and death.

"For the wages of sin is death..." (Rom. 6:23).

And this is simply because we all have sinned. We have not lived up to god's standard of holiness.

"For all have sinned and fall short of the glory of God." (Rom. 3:23).

But, we feel that we have the right to make our own decisions. We deserve "some" fun. We won't stand for being "walked all over" allowing everyone else to get their way. We try to hold on to everything we can get our hands on. We want security! We want "our needs" met! That's only human. But that's the problem. We are too concerned about our "human side." Pride will always stand in the way of God's leading and blessing. We must realize, by the conviction of the Holy Spirit, that we have sinned, missed the mark that God has set. We must want God and His will in our lives more than anything. So what are our forms of idolatry today? An idol is anything that replaces God as our top priority. It could be a relationship, an activity, a dream, materialism, entertainment, pleasures, or just pride, making you the most important. Many Christians today struggle in these areas, trying to find the help and the strength they need to give up their selfish desires. Just as Jesus made it through the valley, He expects us to make it through too. He has promised to help us all the way. As mentioned, the penalty for sin is death, but that wasn't the end of the verse.

"... but the gift of God is eternal life through Jesus Christ, our Lord" (Rom. 6:23b).

We have salvation through Jesus. Now we must unload some of our baggage. We have to be willing to give up on our desires, dreams, comforts, and pleasures. We must empty ourselves of self until all that is left is a spirit willing to do the will of God. Most Christians continue to trip over things of "this" life as they wander through the valley, some never getting to the other side. We can't be crucified with Christ if we can't even get through the Kidron Valley. There is a cross that we must bear, but we will never see that cross if we don't first get through "the valley of the shadow of death." We are reminded of the words of the psalmist, David.

The Valley

"Even though I walk through the valley of the shadow of death, I will fear no evil, for You are with me" (Psalm 23:4).

David knew that no matter what trial or difficulty that he would face that the presence of God would be there to comfort and to guide him. When we are in the presence of God, there is no fear of evil. David was very familiar with the Kidron Valley. He must have crossed it many times. There were probably times that he crossed it while running from his overzealous son, Absalom, or King Saul, who both tried to take his life. But God was with him to give him peace. There were probably times when he crossed it as the commander of his army preparing to conquer with an enemy ready to wipe him out. There were times when death was looming around him. It must have been scary to cross through this huge graveyard, especially at night. In spite of the "shadow of death," David was fearless. He was able to draw upon the strength of the Lord his God. Jesus was fearless as He crossed this valley as well. He looked forward to what was on the other side. Let's consider the passage that is found in Hebrews chapter 12.

Therefore, since we are surrounded by such a great cloud of witnesses, let us throw off everything that hinders and the sin that so easily entangles. And let us run with perseverance the race marked out for us, fixing our eyes on Jesus, the pioneer and perfecter of faith. For the joy set before him he endured the cross, scorning its shame, and sat down at the right hand of the throne of God. Consider him who endured such opposition from sinners, so that you will not grow weary and lose heart. In your struggle against sin, you have not yet resisted to the point of shedding your blood. And have you completely forgotten this word of encouragement that addresses you as a father addresses his son? It says, "My son, do not make light of the Lord's discipline, and do not lose heart when he rebukes you" because the Lord disciplines the one he loves, and he chastens everyone he accepts as his son." Endure hardship as discipline; God is treating you as his children. For what children are not disciplined by their father? If you are not disciplined—and everyone undergoes discipline—then you are not legitimate, not true sons and daughters at all. Moreover, we have all had human fathers who disciplined us and we respected them for it. How much more should we submit to the Father of spirits and live! They disciplined us for a little while as they thought best; but God disciplines us for our good, in order that we may share in his holiness. No discipline seems pleasant at the time, but painful. Later on, however, it produces a harvest of righteousness and peace for those who have been trained by it. Therefore, strengthen your feeble arms and weak knees. "Make level paths for your feet," so that the lame may not be disabled, but rather healed. Make every effort to live in peace with everyone and to be holy; without holiness no one will see the Lord. See to it that no one falls short of the grace of God and that no bitter root grows up to cause trouble and defile many. See that no one is sexually

immoral, or is godless like Esau, who for a single meal sold his inheritance rights as the oldest son. Afterward, as you know, when he wanted to inherit this blessing, he was rejected. Even though he sought the blessing with tears, he could not change what he had done" (Heb. 12:1-17).

In verse 1 we realize that we are not in this thing alone. Not only is God with us, as He was with David and all His people, but we all have to go through this valley. There are those that have made it through the valley and are there to encourage others to make it through as well. But, we must free ourselves of the entanglements of the sinful life. We may not consider ourselves as "sinful," but, there are things in all of our lives that are a hindrance to doing all that God would want us to do. You can't run or even walk when you are burdened down with the cares and pleasures of this life. We've got a lot of "baggage." We are carring around things that weigh us down and keep us from moving forward. We have things such as: unforgiveness, resentment, guilt, poor self-image, insecurities, lust, pride, fear, and the list goes on. We have to let it all go. Bury it once and for all. It takes a persistence everyday to push through the temptations and selfish tendencies. Verse 2 gives us the key to success. It's your focus. Keep looking ahead. There is a goal to reach, a prize to win, and a new life to enjoy. We are following Jesus, so it makes sense to keep our eyes on Him. Look to Him in prayer. Trust Him for direction and provision. He will give you strength and wisdom as you journey along through this life. Jesus looked forward to death. He could see far beyond the cross to the time that He would sit down at the right hand of the Father, having completely fulfilled His divine purpose. Is that your perspective? It would certainly help to focus on what's ahead. It's always good to get a glimpse of the prize that we are working towards. May God give you a glimpse of Heaven that makes this whole journey worth every step. With our eyes and thoughts on Jesus, we will not grow weary or complacent. Discouragement will be replaced by His joy that becomes our strength. Verses 4 through 6 tell us that it's not going to be easy; in fact it will cost you your life! God must discipline us all along the way. He does it because He loves us. Just like parents love their own children. We are His children! We must accept and endure these disciplines from the Lord, as difficult as they may seem to be at times, if we are going to be truly His child. Verse 9 tells us that as we accept these disciplines from God, then we learn to respect Him and begin to discover that new life that He has planned for all of us. Then the writer describes the kind of life that results from yielding to the disciplines of our Heavenly Father. It is a life of holiness, righteousness, and peace. Now that's something worth working towards. It is clearly stated that without this kind of holy life no man can ever see God. The passage gives us the necessary insight as to how to accomplish this task.

    We must strengthen our feeble arms and weak knees. This is an Old Testament term referring to being prepared for the coming of the Lord (Isaiah 35:3). We must continue to do the good that we know that we should do for one another. Our arms can not only carry the weight of our own burdens, but we can also help carry the burdens, cares, and needs of others. Then we can bring them to God, our burden-bearer and trust Him for the answer. We must continue on our knees in prayer daily for the strength and direction that we need from God. Then we must walk the straight path, not going places and doing things that are inconsistent with God's laws or plans for our lives. We must also live at peace with others, not in

The Valley

conflict with them, accusing, ridiculing, or criticizing them, but endeavoring to live a holy and peace-filled life. It goes on to tell us what things to avoid. First of all, don't miss out on the grace of God by not confessing your sin and asking for His forgiveness. Secondly, don't become bitter because of your situation, circumstances, lack of opportunity, treatment from other people, or lack of fulfillment of your wishes and desires. Then, don't be sexually immoral, but pure before God. You must abstain and refrain from any physical gratification that is outside of the marriage covenant. Sex was designed by God for married couples (a man and a woman) to enjoy, bring them closer together emotionally, uniting them as one in the sight of God, and for the procreation of the next generation. And finally, don't be godless or desire earthly things more than heavenly things. That is such a broad statement that only God can speak to you about what that really means in your life. If we do these things that we are not supposed to be doing the result is devastating. No matter how much we beg and plead, we cannot receive God's blessing when we live this kind of life contrary to His Word. There is no second chance when we stand before Him at the end of our lives. We must live our lives today in the light of the eternity awaiting us all. So, we must face this valley fearlessly, with a willingness and determination to get through to the other side, with the help of God.

This valley is not unlike the dessert that the people of God in the Old Testament had to go through. The Israelites were miraculously set free from their slavery in Egypt and brought to a "promise land." However, though they could have made the journey in a matter of days, it took them 40 years of wandering in the wilderness before they actually entered in. It could take someone 40 years to walk across their valley if they are like the Israelites of old. God was leading through His servant, Moses, but most of the people didn't want to follow his leading. They grumbled and complained and wanted to go back to an easier life back in Egypt even though they were slaves. They were willing to trade their freedom and the blessings of God for simple provision such as food and shelter. Maybe that was not as bad as Esau mentioned in the earlier passage who traded God's blessings in for a mere bowl of soup. Many Christians today are content to live a life of ease while they give in to the bondage of the enemy in certain areas of their lives. They don't want to accept the disciplines of the Lord and give up their earthly riches and pleasures. So they wander through the valley of dead man's bones pretending that everything is fine. They are just like the religious leaders of Jesus' day, who He labeled "white-washed tombs. They were pure and clean on the outside, but inside, in their heart, they were full of dead bones and impurity. People like this have lost their focus and will never discover the cross that leads to the "new life." All but two people out of the thousands of Israelites that came out of Egypt died in the wilderness without ever seeing the promise land. Joshua and Caleb were men of faith and continued to believe God even in the face of great opposition. God rewards the faithful! If you are wandering through this Christian life trying to "live right," and trying to overcome the obstacles of the valley, struggling to give up the attractions and entrapments of this world, then it's time to move on! He didn't intend for you to live in the valley of death and defeat. There is a mount to climb. But, ONLY with the help of the Spirit of God can you overcome this valley. If we will trust Him for strength and guidance and if we heed His Word we can continue the marvelous journey of following Him. So, trust Him, rely on Jesus every step of the way. It will get tougher before it gets better. But, IT WILL BE WORTH IT!!!

The Valley

Summary Points

- We all have to cross the valley of self-denial, giving up the things of this world that are not pleasing to God.

- We must decide to bury our pride and selfish pleasures, never to dig them up again. Pride will always stand in the way of God's leading and blessings.

- We must allow the Holy Spirit to open our eyes to the things in our own lives that are not God's will or in His plan for us.

- Once you bury the idols in your life, you will be eligible for God's blessings.

- We must, like Jesus, empty ourselves of self until there's nothing left but a spirit willing to do the will of God.

- God wants to, has promised to, and will, help you to get through this valley.

Death Of A Man

Personal Reflections

(Read I Peter 1:13-22)

1. What are the obstacles that are in your way as you cross this valley?

2. What are the things in you life that you must bury in this valley?

3. What are the changes that you must make in your daily life in order to continue on this journey?

4. Who do you know that could walk alongside you and help you to overcome?

5. What is keeping you from fully relying on God?

6. What will be the benefits from getting through this valley? Is it worth it?

3

The Judgment

A judgment day will come for all of us (Heb. 9:27). Jesus was drug out of the garden, marched across the Kidron Valley, and brought before a religious tribunal. When it was time for Jesus to face His accusers, He was not taken by surprise or unprepared. The religious leaders wanted to rid themselves of this Jesus who had become very popular. They brought Him before Annas, the Father-in-law of Caiaphas, the High Priest. Then they dragged Him into the house of Caiaphas. God had already placed the idea in the mind of Caiaphas that it would be good to have one person die for the people, a human sacrifice. He was frustrated when Jesus would not answer the false accusations made against Him. Finally he asked Jesus if He was the Christ, the Son of God. When Jesus said, "Yes," Caiaphas went into a rage. He obviously did not believe Him, so he was ready to pronounce judgment on Him. The chief priests and the religious ruling body, the Sanhedrin, conspired to put Jesus to death (Matt. 26:59). However, based on their religious laws, they didn't have any grounds to put Him to death so they sent

Death Of A Man

Him to Governor Pilate. When the people brought the false accusations against Jesus before Pilate, Jesus again answered not a word. Jesus could have amazed him with His words of profound truth and mystery as He did when he spoke with such authority to the religious leaders so many times in the past. He could have called in the power of Heaven and God, His father to rescue Him, but He chose not to. Jesus knew that His time had come. He yielded to the Father's master plan and fulfilled the prophecy of Isaiah hundreds of years earlier.

> *"He was oppressed and afflicted yet He opened not his mouth; He was led like a lamb to the slaughter, and as a sheep before his shearers is silent, so He did not open His mouth" (Isaiah 53:7).*

Pilate could not see any validity in the accusations but the crowd was persistent. When Pilate heard that Jesus was from Galilee, he tried to pass the case on to King Herod who happened to be in Jerusalem that day. So then they escorted Jesus into Herod's presence. Herod was anxious to see Jesus because he had heard about the miracles He performed. He had hoped to see one for himself. But when Jesus gave no answer to all his questions, he just began to mock Him and then sent Him right back to Pilate. Pilate tried several times to have Jesus just beaten and released, but the crowd would not be satisfied. Pilate had Jesus flogged or scourged as they called it. In those days that meant a severe beating with a cat-of-nine-tails. This whip would usually have small chunks of metal or glass tied to the end of the leather straps which would gouge into a man's skin. A normal beating of 39 lashes was enough to kill many people, yet Jesus endured it without resistance. Afterwards the soldiers punched Him in the face repeatedly and mocked the

The Judgment

Son of God. They pushed a crown of thorns down on top of His head. By this time, Jesus was hardly recognizable from the beating and abuse He received. These religious leaders, "upstanding model citizens," insisted that because Jesus claimed to be the Son of God, then He must die (John 19:7). Evidently, the Son of God is not welcome on this planet. They would not give up until they saw Him dead, executed, crucified, like a violent criminal. The chief priests stirred the crowd up almost to the point of a riot. There was an annual custom in those days that a prisoner could be released by the wishes of the people. Pilate thought that they would possibly choose Jesus and the case could be over. However rather than having Jesus released and set free, the people chose Barabbas, who was one of the leaders of a rebellion against the Roman rule, as well as a thief and a murderer. So Pilate asked them what they wanted to do with this Jesus and they all cried out, "Crucify Him!" When Pilate realized that the persistence of the crowd was not subsiding, he finally decided to sentence Jesus to death by crucifixion.

Why Jesus? What would anybody have against Jesus, the Son of God, especially the religious leaders? The answer is simple. It was God's plan and it was Satan's desire. That's probably the only time they ever agreed on something. The religious leaders had a very self-centered approach to religion and to Jesus. So, they were angered at His preaching, jealous of His popularity, envious of His power, and fearful of His potential. Satan stirred these human emotions within these men to the point of hatred. They despised Jesus.

Let's take a closer look as to why. First of all, they were angered at His preaching. Jesus' controversial message greatly upset the religious leaders. As Jesus taught with unmatched authority, speaking out against injustice and hypocrisy, the religious people of the day took offense. He came down especially hard on the Pharisees, the religious leaders. The entire 23rd chapter of Matthew's gospel records Jesus' stern rebuke of the Pharisees. He flat-out calls them hypocrites, more than a half-a-dozen times. He called them blind fools, greedy, self-indulgent snakes, ignorant, selfish, two-faced, wicked vipers. Sounds like He didn't appreciate the "religious" example that they were trying to set. They were proud and arrogant and more concerned with judging others than in keeping the law themselves. The fact is that everything looked good from the outside. But God looks on the heart. He can see the motives, intents, and desires inside all of us, that no one else could see. I wonder what He would say about the religious people of today?

Then, they were jealous of His popularity. Jesus had quite a following. Not hundreds, but thousands of people would gather to hear Him teach and perform miracles. They loved Him! The crowds were ready to hail Him as King! That would make any ruler jealous and fearful. Jesus was becoming the voice of "Truth" and "Righteousness." The Pharisees were about to lose their authority, their prominence in society, their power of influence, and their validity as spiritual leaders. They were mad alright. They worried about their effectiveness to rule the people, their control of the laws and rituals, as well as the security of their own lives and lifestyles.

Third, they were envious of His power. They had worked hard their whole lives to get to where they were. Now, some young prophet from Nazareth was moving in on their territory. They tried their best to trick Him and to trap Him into saying something against the laws of the land. But He always turned the tables on them. He spoke with such authority that they felt inferior. His answers continued to surprise them and confound them. He always had the upper hand and they burned with envy.

The Judgment

Finally, they were fearful of His potential. They couldn't see where this was going (maybe if they had, they wouldn't have been so worried). Jesus was building momentum. His popularity was escalating. Considering the numbers of His following, a violent takeover was not out of the question. Their insecurity began to run rampant. However, they were not the type of people to just stand around and watch their world come crashing down before them.

They were going to take action! Right or wrong, they had to do something. Killing Jesus seemed to be the only solution and answer to all their problems. So they carried out their poorly devised plan.

So here's how the last few days of Jesus' life played out.

- He was betrayed by Judas, one of His own followers.
- He was captured like a criminal by a religious mob.
- He was falsely accused by misinformed witnesses.
- He was not believed by Caiaphas, the High Priest.
- He was physically abused by the temple guards.
- He was mocked by King Herod.
- He was rejected and denied by His own followers.
- He was interrogated and threatened by Pilot.
- He was whipped and beaten by the Roman soldiers.
- He was despised by the crowd.
- He was humiliated before the whole world.
- He was sentenced to death by demand of the religious.
- He was nailed to a cross of crucifixion.

You talk about a bad day! Jesus knew what suffering was all about from first-hand experience. The hurt and the pain was real, outwardly as well as inwardly. It was excruciating physically and emotionally, yet Jesus seemed to take it all in stride. There seemed to be a peace that resided within Him through this whole ordeal. It seemed as if He knew it was coming all along. Jesus reaction to it all was not typical, but it did provide a blueprint for all His followers.

Throughout His trial and persecution, Jesus was:

- At peace with God's plan for His Life
  (in spite of the pain and suffering).

- Understanding of other's role in fulfilling God's plan
  (not being judgmental).

- Patient in persecution, not retaliating
  (not demanding His own rights).

- Enduring in suffering for the sake of others
  (and the sake of the eternal Kingdom).

- Forbearing the shame and pain out of love for others
  (and for the glory yet to come).

- Proclaiming the truth in the midst of adversity
  (in spite of the consequences).

That's how Jesus overcame His enemies. That's why Jesus was victorious in the end. We will not go through all that Jesus did, but we can be overcomers in our own particular situations if we follow the blueprint that Jesus laid out for us.

Knowing God's will and His plan enables us to withstand adversity. Jesus would give His life, but not without much pain

The Judgment

and suffering. While still in the garden, His resolved before God, the Father was, "Not my will, but Yours be done." That is why He said to Peter at the time of His arrest, "Shall I not drink the cup the Father has given me?" Drinking "the cup" meant that He had to put aside His humanity, fleshly desires, and human tendencies, in order to do God's will. Our human tendencies will always try to avoid pain, sorrow, rejection, and death. Yet, sometimes, we have to experience those things if we are going to do the will of our Heavenly Father. Jesus asked James and John if they were willing to drink the same "cup," in order to be glorified in heaven (Matt. 20:22). Jesus prophesied in the very next verse, "you will drink it," meaning that they would come to the place in their lives that they would put God ahead of their own humanity. They would be martyred for the cause of Christ.

Now it's your time for judgment. Are you willing to drink "the cup?" Are you willing to suffer for the sake of Christ and His Kingdom and do the will of God? If you are then, you will have to follow Jesus' blueprint, His example of dealing with suffering. If you do, you may experience some of the same consequences that Jesus did. Be aware that some of your friends may leave you and some of your loved ones may reject or betray you. Even religious people may not understand you or even abuse you. You may experience pain, loneliness, humiliation, and persecution.

However, God promises to be with you and see you through all the trials of life. He gives comfort along with His command.

> *"Teaching them to observe all things whatsoever I have commanded you: and, lo, I am with you always, even unto the end of the world. Amen" (Matt. 28:20).*

You must come to know the same peace that Jesus had. Jesus speaks peace to us through His word.

> *"Peace I leave with you, My peace I give to you, not as the world gives. Let not your heart be troubled" (John 14: 27).*

Don't worry! He's got this. He's in control and He knows what He's doing. In fact, all wisdom comes from God. He is the Master of the Universe. He knows what's best for you! Later He closed that discourse with an encouragement,

> *"I have told you these things, so that in me you may have peace. In the world you will have trouble, but take heart! I have overcome the world! (John 16:33).*

The Psalmist, David, realized that the steps of the righteous (God's children) are ordered by the Lord (Psalm 37:23). We must realize that God is in control and we must rest in that fact. When we trust him we can realize what Paul wrote in his letter to the Philippians.

> *Do not be anxious about anything, but in everything, by prayer and petition, with thanksgiving, present your requests to God. And the peace of God, which transcends all understanding, will guard your hearts and your minds in Christ Jesus (Phil. 4:6, 7).*

So don't look around. Look up! We must also understand that God is in control of everybody else. Jesus told Pilate, who was in control.

The Judgment

"You would have no power over me if it were not given to you from above" (John 19:11).

God is in control of the righteous and the ungodly as well. He doesn't force anyone to do anything, good or bad. But He always knows what's going to happen and He always works out His will, in His way, and in His time. So we don't need to stand in judgment of others. Sometimes their bad things are exactly what God uses for His good. Who knew that when Joseph's brothers sold him into slavery that he would become the Prince of Egypt and actually save them from starvation? That's just one of hundreds of stories where God turns something which appears to be bad into something wonderful. When bad things happen to us, we must learn to accept them as God's will and perhaps the source of God's future blessing. We must exercise patience and long-suffering which are attributes of God's Spirit that He has put within us. Your suffering may directly or indirectly benefit someone else or perhaps many people. We don't know what eternal value that our suffering will produce. Suffering is much easier to handle and experience when love is our motivation. Love for God and others will help us to endure. Just as a mother endures the pain of child-birth, the love for her newborn enables her to endure and even forget much of her suffering. There is something beyond our comprehension on the other side of our suffering. Endure to the end and you will receive your reward.

"Blessed is the man who preserves under trial, because when he has stood the test, he will receive the crown of life that God has promised to those who love Him" (James 1:12).

Don't you know that God always keeps His promises! Paul made it clear to us that the suffering that we go through just can't compare with the reward that God has in store for us.

> ***"For I reckon that the sufferings of this present time are not worthy to be compared with the glory which shall be revealed in us (Rom. 8:18).***

Finally, in order to follow Jesus' blueprint for handling suffering, we must be proactive. We must proclaim the truth no matter what the cost. In the midst of persecution or adversity, whether it makes us popular or prosperous, we must tell the truth. God's Word is truth. Know it, speak it, live it. Peter tells us in his first letter to the churches that trials are to be expected.

> ***"Dear friends, do not be surprised at the painful trial you are suffering, as though something strange were happening to you. But rejoice that you participate in the sufferings of Christ, so that you may be overjoyed when His glory is revealed (I Peter 4:12, 13).***

That takes it to a completely new level. Be happy about your suffering? Yes! Look ahead to what might be the end result. Peter wrote earlier in that same chapter that the suffering can even help you to learn to overcome sin in your life. Jesus suffered, but He did not complain.

> ***"To this you were called, because Christ suffered for you, leaving you an example, that you should follow in His steps. He committed no sin, and no deceit was found in His mouth.***

The Judgment

When they hurled their insults at Him, He did not retaliate; when He suffered, He made no threats. Instead, He entrusted Himself to Him (God, the Father) who judges justly (I Peter 2:21- 23).

Jesus put it in God's hands. What about you? Trouble will come, but God will see you through. Jesus is the source of our peace. Jesus is our example, encourager, and our victory. Do you believe it? Can you trust Him, completely? If so, let's continue to follow in His steps to a victorious life!

Summary Points

- Jesus suffering was not only our substitute, but it was also our example. He has given us a blueprint to follow.

- Others may become angry or jealous of those who follow Jesus, as they did Him.

- We must find the peace of God in the midst of our suffering.

- When bad things happen to us, we must learn to accept them as God's will and perhaps the source of God's future blessings.

- We must proclaim God's truth no matter what the consequence.

- We need to learn to rejoice in our suffering realizing that the end result is a great benefit to us and others.

The Judgment

Personal Reflections
(Read I Peter 4:1-19)

1. Are you seeking your own popularity and power? This will cause you to resent Jesus and His teachings as it did the Pharisees.

2. In what areas of your life can you evaluate to make sure that it's "not about YOU?"

3. Can you relate to the sufferings of Jesus in your own life? Was it for the sake of the Kingdom of God?

4. In what ways, specifically, have you suffered for Jesus?

5. What was your initial reaction to your times of suffering? Were you able to follow Jesus' example (His blueprint)?

6. What will your approach be in the future in anticipation of your suffering as a Christian?

4

The Road

So you want to follow Jesus! The road that He walked in order to accomplish His mission was the road to Calvary. The literal road known as the Via Dolorosa, which means, "the sorrowful road," led to a hill just outside the city of Jerusalem. The hill was called "Golgotha" in Hebrew and "Calvary" in Latin, both which mean, "The skull." The road was not that long, but for Jesus it was an agonizing journey. Part of the way was narrow, where He virtually walked alone. His family and friends had abandoned Him. But this was something He had to do alone. Part of the road widened, where on-lookers cried and jeered as He passed by. By custom, Jesus carried His own cross, in spite of His weakened condition. He staggered and fell under the weight of the cross. It was more than He could handle within His physical strength. It must have felt like the "weight of the world" was on His back. And well, in the spiritual sense, it was. Jesus carried the weight or penalty of the world's sin to Calvary's mount. A man named, Simon, was ordered to carry the cross as soldiers hurried Jesus on down the road. Jesus fell several more times out of pure physical exhaustion, but the soldiers continued to prod Him on like "a lamb" going to slaughter. Just as Isaiah, the prophet, had prophesied, Jesus was to become the sacrificial lamb.

> *"Surely he hath borne our griefs, and carried our sorrows: yet we did esteem him stricken, smitten of God, and afflicted. But he was wounded for our transgressions, he was bruised for our iniquities: the chastisement of our peace was upon him; and with his stripes we are healed" (Isaiah 53:4-6).*

All of us have sinned, disobeyed God's laws and commands. We have displeased God by our thoughts and actions. We did not and could never measure up to the standard that God has set for His creation, man. Because of our sin, God demands a price to be paid for that sin to be atoned for. To atone means to make amends. Atonement is the process by which our sins and transgressions are forgiven. God required a life to be taken to satisfy the penalty of sin, disobedience and defiance. Moses implemented the laws of God in the early stages of man's history. God required sacrifices by the people to make up for their sins. The people would sacrifice different animals to make atonement and appease God. An animal had to be slaughtered and its blood spilt.

> *"When Moses had proclaimed every commandment of the law to all the people, he took the blood of calves, together with water, scarlet wool and branches of hyssop, and sprinkled the scroll and all the people. He said,*

The Road

> *This is the blood of the covenant which God has commanded you to keep. In the same way, he sprinkled with the blood both the tabernacle and everything used in its ceremonies. In fact, the law requires that nearly everything be cleansed with blood, and without the shedding of blood there is no forgiveness" (Heb. 9:19-22).*

It is the blood that covers over sin. Jesus knew that He must shed His own blood as the once and for all sacrifice for the sins of all men.

> *"Unlike the other high priests, He does not need to offer sacrifices day after day, first for His own sins, and then for the sins of the people. He sacrificed for their sins once for all when He offered Himself (Heb. 7:27).*

Jesus is our personal sacrifice! He is our substitute! Even though Paul points out that we all have fallen short of God requirements, thankfully that was not the whole story. Let's look at the rest of the story.

> *"For all have sinned and fall short of the glory of God and are justified freely by His grace through the redemption that came by Christ Jesus. God presented him as a sacrifice of atonement, through faith in His blood. He did this to demonstrate His justice, because in His forbearance He had left the sins committed beforehand unpunished, He did it to demonstrate His justice at the present time, so as to be just and the one who justifies those who have faith in Jesus" (Rom. 3:23-26).*

Death Of A Man

It simply states that we are sinners, but we can have our sins forgiven, not by being "good," or by doing "right," but only by putting our faith, hope, and trust in the blood that Jesus shed for our sins. By God's grace, He sent Jesus to be the sacrifice of atonement for all our sins. He did that to not only demonstrate His love for us, but to also demonstrate that He is just. He gave us another chance, an opportunity to be "saved" from the punishment of our sins. His sacrifice justifies us if we believe and have faith in Jesus. Justification simply means that it's as if we had never sinned. When we allow Jesus' blood to wash our sins away, then God no longer sees our sin, but He sees us pure and clean, cleansed by the blood of His precious Son, Jesus. That is the only way we could ever stand in His presence.

Not only would Jesus battle the pain and fatigue physically, but He also faced severe emotional distress. The hostile mob ridiculed Him mercilessly. Maybe even some of the same people were those who cheered His triumphant entrance into Jerusalem just days earlier. Some were weeping uncontrollably in great sorrow. His followers, probably more shocked than anything, stood by helplessly as they watched their Messiah publicly humiliated. Their faith was shaken and their hopes shattered. Then He saw His mother along the roadside. As if His heart was not already broken, He had to deal with the pain and agony that He was putting His own mother through. Jesus' words revealed His heart as He told them not to weep for Him but rather for themselves and their children (Luke 23:28). When we are suffering, are we thinking about others? It was a road of loneliness, ridicule, and suffering.

That is the same road that is in front of you, if you really want to follow Jesus. It's not an easy road. It's not the well-traveled road, or the "normal" road. It's not the road of ease, comfort, and security. At times, you will feel all alone, like you are the only one on that road. At other times, you will be persecuted, unjustly I might add. Sometimes it may seem that your family or friends are of no use to you. Jesus warned us that trouble would come. You will have suffering, maybe physically, or emotionally, or both. There is a cross to bear. Jesus told His disciples the key to being a Christian. Remember the key text of chapter 1.

"If anyone would come after Me, he must deny himself and take up his cross and follow me (Matt. 16:24).

Mark recorded the exact same words. (Mark 8:34) And Luke, who also wrote the book of Acts, wrote those exact words of Jesus in his gospel (Luke 9:23) adding only the word "daily" in his text. Maybe a little word, but it has a great and profound impact to the message. It is a daily decision, a daily activity, a day by day walk. What does it mean to deny yourself? What does it mean to take up your cross? That is what we must know if we are to follow Jesus! Jesus used the term "deny" which is translated from a few different words in the original Greek. He did not use the term that meant to refuse yourself. He used rather the term that meant to disown yourself. Jesus was not telling us to deny ourselves life, sustenance, or our daily needs. Rather He was saying that if you want to be follower of Mine, you must give up your right to yourself, control of your life, ownership. Once you have given God control of and authority over your life then He says you must take up your cross.

You must learn to be selfless, void of "self," and not selfish. We live in a very selfish world. The fact is that we grow up selfish. We want what we want, when we want it, or we are going to cry and scream until we get it. And I am not just talking about little babies. We have a lot of "big babies" in our society. People that demand to have it their way. Many people are controlling, they not only want control of their own lives, but they want to control others as well. They want to tell them what they should do, how they should look, and what they should say. They think that they know best. They want to play "God." We need leaders in our world, but we don't need proud and arrogant people who are just hungry for power and control. Jesus is telling us that we have to yield control of our lives to Him. We must let Him tell us what to do, how to look, and what to say. It's not easy, but with daily practice, prayer, and faith, we can learn to walk on the road of selflessness. Deny that human tendency to want it your way. Deny the human tendency to want to be in control. Take little steps at a time. Just deny yourself a simple pleasure such as sweets or an extra 15 minutes of sleep. Then work towards bigger and bigger sacrifices. Make it a habit of thinking about "the other person" more than yourself. Put yourself in their shoes. Live to please and serve others, striving to meet their needs. Allow your needs to take a "back seat." You can't just ignore them completely. There are certain needs that should and must be tended to, but they don't have to scream, "gimme, gimme, gimme." We have to take control and then give control. You can't give someone control of something that you don't have control of yourself. Many influences attempt to control you. Aside from certain people, there is the media, our society, which tries to tell you how you ought to live your life. Behind all that is the Devil, who wants to control you without you even knowing it. If he can get you to believe that you are, and rightfully so, in control of your life and you know what's best for you, then he's got you right where he wants you. He's really in control through your sinful nature. But if we yield ourselves to God, He will give us a new nature, one of righteousness.

But even then, there is a battle going on inside us between the two natures. This war raging on in our spirit will be

The Road

discussed in detail in a later chapter. Right now, we must be simply commit our hearts and lives to Jesus and give Him full control.

That suggests that you must not allow your wants and desires to dominate or dictate your life and daily decisions. You must surrender your life, your hopes, your dreams, and your plans to God's control. You must give God total authority over your entire life. That is the complete opposite of the humanistic philosophy of the western culture today. We live in a culture where we are taught to get all we can for ourselves. "Take control of your life." "Fulfill your dreams!" "Do your own thing." But Jesus said to give it all up for Him. Jesus said, "Follow Me." (not this world). The road is rocky and dirty and lonely, but you can make it. Jesus, who already walked the road is by your side. He left a trail of blood all along the road to Calvary. We must follow that trail; it will lead us to victory. It's not easy, but God's grace and power will sustain you if you trust Him as the Apostle Paul did.

> ***And he said unto me, My grace is sufficient for thee: for my strength is made perfect in weakness. Most gladly therefore will I rather glory in my infirmities, that the power of Christ may rest upon me. Therefore I take pleasure in infirmities, in reproaches, in necessities, in persecutions, in distresses for Christ's sake: for when I am weak, then am I strong (II Cor. 12: 9, 10).***

He will give you the strength you need and lead you every step of the way. The road Jesus traveled ended in heaven. If we want to follow Him and end up there too, we must learn how to deny ourselves and take up our cross, daily!

Death Of A Man

Summary Points

- There are many roads in life to follow, but there is only one road that Jesus took. It leads to Heaven.

- The road to Calvary was rough, lonely, and completely exhausting, but Jesus made it and He will be with us to help us make it.

- The devil wants us to live by human nature, in other words, our sinful nature. That puts him in control.

- Jesus commands those who follow Him to deny themselves. Deny yourself is giving up control of your life and desires. We yield control little by little and day by day.

- Make a habit of putting other people ahead of yourself. Seek to meet their needs.

- Take Up your cross, not matter what the cost.

The Road

Personal Reflections

(Also Read Proverbs 16:1-9, 25)

1. Considering the path that your life is on right now, would Jesus be comfortable walking it with you? (Why, or why not?)

2. Has God placed you on the path that you're on right now, and is He directing your every step?

3. What obstacles will you have to overcome while on your path of righteousness? What does it mean to you to take up your cross?

4. How do you deal with people who don't understand the path you are on? Are you putting others first?

5. What are your immediate and long-term benefits for being on the road that Jesus has called you to walk?

6. What are the things that you are going to have to deal with in order to allow God to have full control in your life?

5

The Cross

We must carry our cross. Jesus said if we don't carry our cross, then we are not worthy of a relationship with Him. We can't be one of His followers without obedience in this matter.

"Anyone who does not take his cross and follow me is not worthy of me" (Matt. 10:38).

What kind of cross must we carry? The cross of Jesus was no ordinary cross. It may have looked like two large and long pieces of wood, but it was so much more. There is only one translation from the original text for the word cross. It is a stake, post, or pole used to carry out capital punishment. It symbolized the death penalty by crucifixion. For us, in the figurative sense, it refers to self-denial, death to self. The cross in those days meant only one thing, "death." It meant a long agonizing death by suffocation. For as one hung on a cross they would have to pull up with their arms and push up with their feet in order to get a breath. Eventually their strength would run out. If it took longer than expected, they would have their legs broken, which would bring about the end, death. It was one of the spectator sports of that time. It was designed for punishment, humiliation, mockery, and torture. The people tried to belittle Jesus and to make Him feel less than a man or even less than human. However, this did not have an effect on Him. You can't humiliate someone who is already humble. Jesus had humbled Himself in the garden, where He figuratively picked up His cross. It was a cross of humility, submission, and servanthood.

Jesus humbled Himself to become a man.

> ***"Let this mind be in you, which was also in Christ Jesus: Who, being in the form of God, thought it not robbery to be equal with God: But made himself of no reputation, and took upon him the form of a servant, and was made in the likeness of men" (Phil. 2:5-7).***

He left the portals of Heaven to come to earth, being born of a virgin, for the distinct purpose of dying on the cross. He knew that this humility would carry a heavy price, a price of rejection, ridicule, and even betrayal. He was rejected by His own people, the Jews, who had longed to see the Messiah, the Deliverer, whom they were about to crucify. Ridicule came from the religious people, the Chief Priests and Pharisees, the rulers of the Temple. They were all blinded to the true identity of Jesus, the Son of God. And yes, even betrayal and denial by His own friends, His disciples. Through all the cursing, beating, mocking, interrogating by the chief priests and soldiers at his trial, Jesus remained calm, unemotional, steadfast. He was willing to carry the cross of humility.

It was a cross of submission. Jesus didn't go through all this because He thought He deserved it, or couldn't do anything about it. He willingly carried His cross out of submission to the will of the Father.

> *"Though he were a Son, yet learned he obedience by the things which he suffered. And being made perfect, he became the author of eternal salvation unto all them that obey him" (Heb. 5: 8,9).*

His Father in Heaven had sent Him on a mission, and Jesus was determined to fulfill it, no matter what it took. Jesus defined submission in the garden when He prayed for the Father's will to be done over His own will and desires. Submission means surrender of oneself to the decisions of another. Paul writes about Jesus' submission to the Father's plan.

> *"And being found in appearance as a man, He humbled Himself and became obedient to death, even death on a cross" (Phil. 2:8).*

King Saul learned the hard way that obedience is better than sacrifice when he tried to offer animal sacrifices to God after he plundered the Amalekites. He did this in disobedience to God because God had already instructed him to completely destroy everything of the Amalekites (I Sam. 15:22). But Saul had his own idea. He wanted to serve God on his own terms. Obedience is not about being creative and coming up with your individual plans. It's following someone else's plan and sometimes and maybe most of the time, obedience is a sacrifice. Jesus bore a cross of obedience and ultimate submission.

It was also a cross of servanthood, servanthood to all

mankind. Jesus carried that cross not only out of humility, submission, and obedience, but He also carried it out of love. Love is what nailed Jesus to the cross; His love for all mankind. Jesus tells us what real love is all about.

> ***"No greater love hath any man than a man lay down his life for his friends" (John 15:13).***

Jesus' love was beyond "greater." He laid down His life for His enemies as well.

> ***"In that while we were yet sinners (enemies of God), Christ died for the ungodly" (Rom. 5:8).***

Jesus loves everyone and He proved it. Jesus taught us how to be a servant. He willingly took upon Himself the sin of the world, and its penalty, death (Romans 6:23). Jesus fed the hungry, healed the sick, washed the disciples feet, forgave the sinner, and then died for them all. He died so they might live.

> ***"Jesus said unto her, I am the resurrection and the life: he that believeth in me, though he were dead, yet shall he live. And whosoever liveth and believeth in me shall never die. Believest thou this?" (John 11:25, 26).***

When Jesus gave His life, it was the greatest act of servanthood known to man.

A cross of humility, submission, and sevanthood, was the cross that Jesus carried. That is the same cross that He asks you to carry. In order to follow Jesus, we must take up our cross, walk down that same road, and lay our lives down. We must be humble before God and within ourselves, eliminating all pride and self-centeredness. We must submit to God as supreme authority by obeying His Word and yielding control of every area of our lives, including our hopes and dreams. And we must become a servant to all, putting others ahead of ourselves and seeking to meet their needs not our own. Jesus said that if we want to be great in His Kingdom, we must be a servant (Matt 20:26). Just before Jesus said take up your cross, He told His disciples that they must forfeit their own lives.

> **"He that loses his life for my sake shall find it"(Mt. 16:25, Mark 8:35, Luke 9:24).**

He wants us to lose our life so He can give us a new one. Jesus didn't come to give us a "better life." He came so that we can have a "new life." In order to experience that life, we must humble ourselves, not valuing our lives and plans over His. We must also serve Him by being a servant to others around us. That's a lot to ask for some people. And that is why so many Christians never experience the victorious overcoming life that God has planned for them. They bail out when the tough times come and never make it down the road to Calvary. They are too proud or self-sufficient to give up the control of their lives. It's a natural desire or craving to want to be "in charge." They become self-absorbed or caught up with the things of this world. Jesus spelled it out clearly in His parable of the sower. Even after people hear the truth about this gospel of salvation, many of them don't follow through with a daily walk of obedience to the Lord. He stated some reasons why when He explained the parable to His disciples.

> **"Listen then to what the parable of the sower means: When anyone hears the message about the kingdom and does not understand it, the evil**

one comes and snatches away what was sown in their heart. This is the seed sown along the path. The seed falling on rocky ground refers to someone who hears the word and at once receives it with joy. But since they have no root, they last only a short time. When trouble or persecution comes because of the word, they quickly fall away. The seed falling among the thorns refers to someone who hears the word, but the worries of this life and the deceitfulness of wealth choke the word, making it unfruitful. But the seed falling on good soil refers to someone who hears the word and understands it. This is the one who produces a crop, yielding a hundred, sixty or thirty times what was sown"(Matt. 13:18-23).

Many times Christians never grow or advance in their faith or walk with the Lord, for various reasons. Jesus generalized some of those reasons in this parable. Sometimes it's just the enemy. The Devil, who seeks to steal, kill, and destroy anything or anyone, that is godly, has robbed many people of the truths they at one time embraced. He is the master deceiver. Truth has to be reinforced many times over for it to take root in some people. So, if a person doesn't continue to go to church and read God's word regularly, then the truths of God will lose their significance and power of influence in their lives. Some people have no reference point for understanding biblical truth. That's called living in darkness. People are not born with a divine understanding of love and forgiveness. It must be learned. When these people hear the truth about God, it sounds good and they are ready to accept it. However, their past does not confirm the same truths and they simply fall back on what they've known their whole lives. Sometimes, as Jesus stated, the things of this world have so much of a hold on some people that they cannot let them go in order to grasp a new way of life. People will desperately hold on to their security as a means of self-preservation. They think that without their money, position, or significant relationship, they will not be able to survive. Jesus said that this attitude will literally choke out the spiritual truths that can transform a life. You have to first be willing to change, before change can happen. In order for the seed of God to grow in you, in takes a complete dependence on Him. Hearing and then understanding that these are truths that must be incorporated into one's own heart and life is the key that makes the difference. It takes faith. That's the starting point for the person with the "good soil." Then it takes action. In the book of James, he writes about faith and works and how they must work hand in hand. Not only does the seed have to find good soil, but it also needs to have sun and rain to grow. We must cultivate the seed of God so that it will produce a harvest of righteousness. Not every seed grows. Many seeds (Christians) never seem to ever produce a crop (or bear fruit).

If that's been you in the past, it doesn't have to be you anymore. If you have not allowed the seed of God to grow in you in the past, then you can change that today. We have all been there at one time or another. The fact is that there has been many a "believer" who made a decision to follow Jesus (in the garden of his heart), but never continued down the road of self-denial. That is why Jesus said in the great *Sermon on the Mount*, that narrow is the gate that leads to eternal life and only a few find it.

> ***"Enter ye in at the strait gate: for wide is the gate, and broad is the way, that leadeth to destruction, and many there be which go in***

> *thereat. But small is the gate and narrow the road that leads to life, and only a few find it" (Matt. 7:13).*

You want to be a part of "the few." A few refers to a small percentage of Christians. And again Jesus refers to "Christians" that never follow Him down this road a few verses later.

> *"Not everyone who says to me, 'Lord, Lord' (believed for salvation) will enter the kingdom of heaven, but only he who does the will of My Father who is in heaven (walk the road of self-denial). Many will say to me on that day, 'Lord, Lord, did we not prophesy in Your Name, and in Your Name drive out demons and perform many miracles?' Then I will tell them plainly, I never knew you. Away from me you evildoers!"(Matt. 7:21-23).*

People can fool you, yes, even so-called Christians. Like the Pharisees of old, they can appear to be "all that" on the outside, but their heart is not right with God. They simply have a form of godliness (II Tim. 3: 1-5). People can confess their sin, profess Jesus as their Savior and even serve in the church without really dying to self, taking up their cross and living in humble obedience to God. You have to have a personal and intimate relationship with Him. You have to be in love with Him, more than anything and anyone else. Just before Jesus said to take up your cross, He reminded us that we need to love Him the most.

> *"Anyone who loves his father or mother more than me is not worthy of me; anyone who loves*

his son or daughter more than me is not worthy of me" (Matt. 10:37).

We must give Him top priority in our lives and consider everything else worthless. Jesus puts everything in perspective.

"What good will it be for a man if he gains the whole world, yet forgets his soul?" (Matt. 16: 26).

When you get to the place in your relationship with the Lord where He is your all in all, your everything, then you will have the same attitude that Paul had.

"But what things were gain to me, those I counted loss for Christ. Yea doubtless, and I count all things but loss for the excellency of the knowledge of Christ Jesus my Lord: for whom I have suffered the loss of all things, and do count them but dung, that I may win Christ, And be found in him, not having mine own righteousness, which is of the law, but that which is through the faith of Christ, the righteousness which is of God by faith: That I may know him, and the power of his resurrection, and the fellowship of his sufferings, being made conformable unto his death" (Phil. 3: 7-10).

You must know Him and love Him. May it never be said to you, "I never knew you!"

Be His faithful follower and servant. When you fall and when you fail, (and you will) just pick yourself up, dust yourself off and keep going. Jesus fell several times on the way to Calvary, but He didn't quit. He kept going. This is not the end, the journey has a destination. There is a cross of humility, submission and servanthood with your name on it. When you pick up your cross, you are enlisting in God's army. We join the fight. It is a war against sin and Satan and his evil influences in this world. This battle will be discussed further as we continue our journey. But know this, God and "Good" will win out in the end; we will win. You can be victorious, so pick up your cross and let's keep following Jesus.

The Cross

Summary Points

- The cross that Jesus carried was a cross of humility, submission, and servanthood.

- We must carry that same cross if we are to follow Jesus.

- Humility ought to be the underlying factor in all we do.

- Submission means yielding your life to the decisions of another.

- Jesus showed us that carrying a cross is all about loving and serving others.

- Not everyone that claims to follow Jesus is willing to carry His cross.

Death Of A Man

Personal Reflections
(Also read Matthew 10:17-39)

1. Have you listened and obeyed? Have you let the seed of God's Word grow inside you?

2. How has your cross affected your personal relationships?

3. In what ways do you show your humility?

4. In what areas of your life have you submitted to the Lord's influence and His will?

5. What are some things that you can do from this day forward to "carry your cross?"

6. What can you do for others, on a daily basis, to be servant of all?

6

The Death

Jesus predicted His own death. He not only told the disciples that He was going to die, but He also told them that they too must follow Him in death.

> *Jesus replied, "The hour has come for the Son of Man to be glorified. Very truly I tell you, unless a kernel of wheat falls to the ground and dies, it remains only a single seed. But if it dies, it produces many seeds. Anyone who loves their life will lose it, while anyone who hates their life in this world will keep it for eternal life. Whoever serves me must follow me; and where I am, my servant also will be. My Father will honor the one who serves me" (John 12:23-26).*

Death Of A Man

The only way to live is to die. Jesus knew that He was the one and only Son of God. But He also knew that if He would die, His death would produce many more sons and daughters of God.

> ***"Yet to all who receive Him, to those who believed in His name, He gave the right to become children of God" (John 1:12).***

God wants a big family! He has an "open door" policy with only one requirement, you must believe and receive His Son, Jesus! God intended for Jesus not to be the one and only, but to simply be the first of many.

> ***"For those God foreknew He also predestined to be conformed to the likeness of His Son, that He might be the first-born among many brothers" (Rom. 8:29).***

If we die like He died, we will live like He lives! God's plan all along was to bring you into "the family!" In order to do that, we have to become like His Son, Jesus. Jesus tells us that the way we do that is to lose our life. We must "hate" our life in this world. In the original text the word means to destroy. We must destroy the old life of worldliness and sin, the sinful nature, so we can embrace the new life that God offers. If you cling to a life of selfishness and materialism, you will not only lose it all in the end, but you will lose your life as well. How will God, the Father, honor those who forsake their own lives to serve Jesus, His Son? I don't know, but whatever it is, I want it. It will be worth it all someday, if we just learn to follow Jesus.

The lonely road to Calvary's mount was finally completed. No more hills to climb, no more miles to walk, no more steps to take. Upon arrival at Golgatha, there was no need for decision.

The Death

Jesus simply fell to His knees and slowly but reverently rolled over onto the cross. His submission to the Father was a direct result of His Gethsemane commitment to Him, "not my will, but yours." As they nailed Him to the cross, hoisted it up and thrust it into place, Jesus was left hanging, suspended between Heaven and Earth. How symbolic! Jesus indeed became a bridge spanning the gap created by sin between God in heaven and man on earth. Jesus literally paid the price for the sins of the world.

> **"For he hath made him to be sin for us, who knew no sin; that we might be made the righteousness of God in Him" (II Cor. 5:21).**

Jesus exchanged places with us. He was righteous and we were sinners. He paid our penalty of sin on the cross and we get to have His righteousness by simply accepting the exchange. Not only did Jesus suffer physically but spiritually as well. He paid the once and for all sacrifice for sin, separating Himself from His Father. He would cry out to God, the Father from the cross.

> **"And about the ninth hour Jesus cried with a loud voice, saying, Eli, Eli, lama sabachthani? that is to say, My God, my God, why hast thou forsaken me?" (Matt. 27:46).**

While Jesus bore the weight of sin, He would experience estrangement from the Father for the first and last time. God, the Father, cannot fellowship (have a relationship with) anyone who is bound up by sin. God, for those few hours, withheld His mercy and grace and His presence from His Son and allowed Him to pay the price and penalty for our sin. Jesus' death was a willing sacrifice of love. Even in His last hours of life He showed concern for others. First, He turned to one of the thieves on His one side, who cried out for mercy. Jesus spoke words of peace to him,

> *"I tell you the truth, today you shall be with Me in Paradise"(Luke 23:43).*

No matter who you are, if you cry out to Jesus for mercy, He will save you.

> *"And everyone who calls on the name of the Lord will be saved" (Joel 2: 32).*

Then Jesus' heart of compassion bled for His mother, as she knelt at the foot of the cross with the beloved disciple, John. Jesus, in spite of much pain and agony, uttered words of comfort to His mother and His beloved friend, John,

"Dear woman, here is your son, and to the disciple, here is your mother" (John 19:26,27).

Jesus was compelled to make sure everyone was cared for. Even His accusers and torturers received compassion from the Lord as He cried out,

> *"Father, forgive them, for they do not know what they are doing" (Luke 23:34).*

True love is being able to forgive, even our enemies.

After six hours on the cross, the body of Jesus was drained of strength. Having realized that He had fulfilled all prophecy and had accomplished the work for which He was sent, He cried out with a loud voice.

The Death

"It is finished" (John 19:30). "Father, into your hands I commit My spirit" (Luke 23: 46).

He still had strength to cry out. He probably could have hung there forever, because He was extremely strong in spirit, but He did what He came to do and it was time to go back home to be with the Father. So, He died. Jesus showed us how to live and He showed us how to die. We must die! We will either die to sin, or we will die in our sins. Jesus said it plainly, as recorded by John, the beloved.

"I told you that you would die in your sins; if you do not believe that I am the one I claim to be, you will indeed die in your sins" (John 8:24).

The psalmist, David tells us how we came to be in this condition.

"Surely I was sinful at birth, sinful from the time my mother conceived me" (Psalm 51:5).

We were born in sin, with a sin-nature. We were slaves to sin, because we sinned naturally without even knowing it. But, sin brings judgment and death, eternal death!

"Know ye not, that to whom ye yield yourselves servants to obey, his servants ye are to whom ye obey; whether of sin unto death, or of obedience unto righteousness?" (Rom. 6:16).

You were a slave. But it was not until the truth of God was revealed, before you realized your fateful state, a sinner. However, if you obey God and His Word, you become a slave to Him and no longer a slave to sin. So, by believing in Him, you have died to sin and no longer have to die (eternally) for your sin.

> ***"For we know that our old self was crucified with Him so that the body of sin might be done away with, that we should no longer be slaves to sin – because anyone who has died has been freed from sin" (Rom. 6:6, 7).***

You will serve someone. You are a slave, but to whom? If you die to sin, you are free from that task-master and free to obey God as your new master. If we believe in Him, we must be crucified with Him. Paul learned this truth and proclaimed to the Christians at Philippi.

> ***"I am crucified with Christ, nevertheless I live, yet not I, but Christ liveth in me, and the life that I now live in the flesh, I live by faith in the Son of God, who loved me and gave Himself for me" (Gal. 2:20).***

This is the thrust of the entire book. We must be crucified with Christ, but not dead. We must die to our self-centered life and live for God with a Christ-centered life. We live by faith in what Jesus did for us because of His great love for us. Paul says to the church in Rome that we, as His followers, have been crucified with Christ. We must die like Jesus died, in humility and submission to the Father. It is a process which includes compassion for friends, associates, and family, as well as forgiveness toward everyone, even our enemies. It is a painful process, but without it we can never accomplish God's will for our lives. We must get to the place where we can cry out the same words as Jesus, "It is finished." We must be finished with the works of the flesh, our own desires and dreams. When we die to self, then we can live for God. Suffering in the body by denying fleshly or worldly desires will help you to be disciplined over the temptation of sin and then you will begin to live you life for God's will and not you own (I Peter 4: 1, 2). Then we can truly say, like Jesus, we commit our spirits into the hands of God. If our lives are in His hands, then we have nothing to fear or worry about. Jesus, Himself, tells us that we are safe.

> *"My sheep listen to My voice; I know them, and they follow Me. I give them eternal life, and they shall never perish; no one can snatch them out of My hand. My Father, who has given them to Me, is greater than all; no one can snatch them out of My Father's hand. I and the Father are one" (John 10:27-30).*

Sheep just follow. They don't argue, debate, complain or criticize. They recognize who is in charge and they trust him. Jesus wants to lead us. He explained, earlier in the chapter, the reason His Father loves Him is because of His sacrifice for you and me.

> *"I am the good shepherd; I know My sheep and My sheep know Me – just as the Father knows Me and I know the Father – and I lay down My life for the sheep. The reason My Father loves Me is that I lay down My life – only to take it up again" (John 10:14, 15, 17).*

If we are tuned into His voice, we will be able to follow where

He's leading. We are safe in His loving arms. He loved us enough to die for us. The Father loves Him because He is His faithful and obedient Son, who was willing to die. He set the example for us. If we love Him enough, then we will be willing to lay our lives down. He will pour out His love on us, as His faithful and obedient children.

When we die, we shall be raised! The apostle Paul relates this process to baptism in Romans chapter 6. Repentance, which is turning from the sin which you have been convicted about, prepares you for baptism. Baptism is a symbolic ritual signifying a change of lifestyle, direction, and authority in your life. It is the cleansing of an old life and the forth-coming of a new life. Baptism thus symbolizes a watery grave, where the old life (of sin) is buried.

> *"Know ye not, that so many of us as were baptized into Jesus Christ were baptized into his death? Therefore we are buried with him by baptism into death: that like as Christ was raised up from the dead by the glory of the Father, even so we also should walk in newness of life. For if we have been planted together in the likeness of his death, we shall be also in the likeness of his resurrection" (Rom. 6:3-5).*

Death brings life, a life that is free from the power of sin. Death to self and sin is a "good thing." The problem today is that too many people want to live the "new life" without dying to the "old life" first. They don't want to deal with their sin and selfishness and therefore never really experience "new life" in Christ. In a letter to the church in Corinth Paul writes about this.

> *"If any man be in Christ, he is a new creation,*

The Death

old things are passed away, and behold, all things have become new" (II Cor. 5:17).

If the old sin-nature is gone and we are dead to self, our whole life, attitudes, and actions will change. You can't tempt, hurt, or offend a dead person. A lot of things that bothered us before simply don't have the same effect on us. We are born again! We have a new life. What is this "new life" like? Well, let's continue on our journey and find out.

Summary Points

- We are all slaves to someone; who are you serving?

- We will either die to sin or die in our sin. The result is two completely different lives and destinations.

- If we die to sin we are free from the control of our sinful nature, and the powerful influence of Satan, and we will receive a new life in Christ.

- If we truly love Jesus, then we will follow His example and lay our lives down for Him.

- Those who belong to Jesus are safe in His hands and the hands of Father, God.

- If we are dead to sin then temptations and offenses against us don't have the same effect on us.

The Death

<u>Personal Reflections</u>

(Also read Ephesians 4: 22-32)

1. What is it in your life that is keeping you from laying your life down in complete surrender?

2. Who is it that you need to forgive before you can die?

3. To whom do you need to show more compassion?

4. What changes are you going to have to make to die daily?

5. What are some things that you look forward to in your new life in Christ?

6. What are the "old things" that were in your life that are now gone? What's new?

7

The Resurrection

The greatest event in all history, the greatest marvel of all time was, on the third day, He arose from the grave. Jesus rose from the dead. The walk by Mary Magdalene and the other Mary to the sepulcher was a lonely one that day. This walk, out of respect and love, was not filled with much anticipation. As they approached the tomb, a rush of thoughts stormed their minds as they saw the stone had been rolled back from the tomb. The stone that was supposed to seal Jesus' fate forever was no match for the angel of God. The angel simply rolled back the stone not to let Jesus out, but to let others in to see the proof for themselves. The angel spoke to the terrified women who had assumed that someone had stolen the body of Jesus.

> *"Don't be afraid, for I know that you are looking for Jesus, who was crucified. He is not here; He has risen just as He said. Come see the place where He lay. Then go quickly and tell His disciples: He has risen from the dead and is*

> *going ahead of you into Galilee. There you will see Him. Now I have told you" (Matt. 28:6,7).*

The women left in complete amazement yet still unsure, until they saw Him face to face. Jesus lovingly showed Himself to Mary, the other disciples, and multitudes of others during the next 40 days. However, Jesus was not the same as they knew Him. He walked and talked with them but He now had a glorified, resurrected body. His body looked the same as He was recognized by many. He ate with the disciples and even encouraged Thomas to feel His hands and side that had been nailed and pierced at the crucifixion. This spiritual body, however, was not bound by humanity nor was it subject to the laws of nature. He was not bound by time or space. Jesus apparently walked through walls as He instantly appeared before the disciples who were gathered behind closed doors. He had no earthly limitations. There was a glory and countenance about Him that revealed His divinity. Jesus had risen with victory over death, hell, and the grave. He is alive!

> *"And if Christ be not risen, then is our preaching vain, and your faith is also vain" (I Cor. 15:14).*

If it hadn't been for the fact of His resurrection, then our religion and beliefs would be worthless. More than just a show of His power, Jesus rose to impart new life to all who would believe. He lives today to enable us to know that same resurrection power that raised Him from the dead. Romans chapter 6 tells us that if we die with Him we shall rise in a newness of life. When Jesus died He destroyed the power of sin. When we die to our sinful nature, that same power of sin is destroyed in our lives. We are no longer in bondage to that power which

The Resurrection

once held us captive. Like the stone that sealed the tomb of Jesus, once the stone of bondage has been rolled away from our lives, we must come out and show ourselves to the world with a new spiritual body. We must show that we are no longer in bondage to sin or controlled by our own humanity. There is now another power that is at work in us known as the power of God or the power of the Spirit of God. Therefore, sin no longer controls your life (Romans 6:14).

> *"If the Spirit of Him who raised Jesus from the dead is living in you, He who raised Christ from the dead will also give life to your mortal bodies through His Spirit, who is in you" (Rom. 8:11).*

We have a new life through the Spirit of God who dwells inside of us. This life that has been given cannot be destroyed. It will live in us forever. This spiritual power enables us to overcome any obstacle in life. Jesus passed on His authority to His disciples.

> *"Behold, I give unto you power to tread on serpents and scorpions, and over all the power of the enemy: and nothing shall by any means hurt you" (Luke 10:19).*

The disciples would use that power to do great things for God. They would perform many miracles and begin to build the Church, the Kingdom of God's people. They were given power to overcome. Jesus tells all His followers the same thing. We can overcome any evil spirit or satanic force by the power of God's Spirit working in and through us. It simply takes faith. Faith in Jesus, the Son of God, who is all-powerful.

Almighty God is the authority that is behind us. It is He that gives us our identity.

> *"For whatsoever is born of God overcometh the world: and this is the victory that overcometh the world, even our faith. Who is he that overcometh the world, but he that believeth that Jesus is the Son of God?" (I John 5:4,5).*

We can overcome anything in this world. The Apostle John writes about the end times and how we overcome Satan, himself.

> *"And they overcame him by the blood of the Lamb, and by the word of their testimony; and they loved not their lives unto the death" (Rev. 12:11).*

When we believe in Jesus and confess Him as Lord, we have overcoming power. We are not subject to the influences and evil forces of this world. We are above that. We can live righteously and victoriously every day.

We don't have to live in defeat and discouragement. We are overcomers. We don't have to just survive "under the circumstances." We should be living "above the circumstances." When we realize the power that is at work in us and see things from an eternal perspective, we will learn to live in "victory" everyday. God has promised to continue working in and through your life all your days.

> *"Being confident of this, that He who began a good work in you will carry it on to completion until the day of Christ Jesus" (Phil. 1:6).*

God is at work in you. What more could you ask for. Let His power strengthen you. Let His Spirit guide you. Let Him do great things in your life. Be confident, you have nothing to fear. God is not only with us, but He is in us. He promised to give us everything that we need to live for Him in victory.

> *"According as his divine power hath given unto us all things that pertain unto life and godliness, through the knowledge of him that hath called us to glory and virtue" (II Peter 1:3).*

We have been given all that we need to live victorious in this life by the Spirit of God that lives within us. He gives us power, talents, abilities, opportunities, wisdom, and special gifts. As we are sensitive to His leading we can operate in His power and be successful in any area of life. God has given special gifts and talents to His children for the purpose of working together to build His Kingdom here on earth. There are many different gifts and types of gifts or talents that He uses to encourage, teach, and build up the "Body of Christ," the church.

> *"But to each one of us grace has been given as Christ apportioned it...to prepare God's people for works of service, so that the body of Christ may be built up" (Eph. 4:7,12).*

We are all members of His "body" and Jesus Christ is the Head. All the different parts of the body are equally important in working together as one. Jesus had a job for Peter to do and Paul and me and you. We must find out what our role is in serving God and do it without fear, with all our might. Jesus would spend his last few days telling His disciples what their task would be. In Matthew 28:18-20, He told them to build the church, a gathering of believers, and teach them everything that they had learned from Him. He assured them that He would be with them, always, through His Spirit.

Jesus was always calming their fears when He came into their presence. He still brings that same peace to us today. Jesus took time to restore Peter back into a right relationship after he had denied even knowing Jesus on the night He was arrested. He encouraged him and commissioned him for the work He had planned for him to do. The only thing Jesus needed to know was if he really loved Him more than anything.

> *"So when they had dined, Jesus saith to Simon Peter, Simon, son of Jonas, lovest thou me more than these? He saith unto him, Yea, Lord; thou knowest that I love thee. He saith unto him, Feed my lambs. He saith to him again the second time, Simon, son of Jonas, lovest thou me? He saith unto him, Yea, Lord; thou knowest that I love thee. He saith unto him, Feed my sheep. He saith unto him the third time, Simon, son of Jonas, lovest thou me? Peter was grieved because he said unto him the third time, Lovest thou me? And he said unto him, Lord, thou knowest all things; thou knowest that I love thee. Jesus saith unto him, Feed my sheep"* (John 21: 15-17).

Later Jesus simply told Peter to "follow" Him. The only prerequisite to serving Jesus in the Kingdom of God is to answer that one question, "Do you love Jesus?" That is all Jesus is concerned with, your heart. He made that clear when He told the Pharisees what is really the most important commandment of all.

> *"Master, which is the great commandment in the law? Jesus said unto him, Thou shalt love the Lord thy God with all thy heart, and with all thy soul, and with all thy mind. This is the first and great commandment. And the second is like unto it, Thou shalt love thy neighbor as thyself. On these two commandments hang all the law and the prophets" (Matt. 22: 36-40).*

If you love Jesus with everything that is in you, then you are ready to serve Him, to follow Him.

Then, after 40 days Jesus ascended back into Heaven. His glorification resulted in Him being seated at the right hand of the Father in Heaven. From there He will reign and of His Kingdom there will be no end (Isaiah 9:7). When we follow Jesus all the way, our fate will be the same. We will also spend eternity in the presence of God, the Father. We will even reign with Him (Rev. 2:26). He's coming back for us. We will be in heaven with Jesus forever, just as He promised. Jesus' promise to His disciples is for us as well.

> *"Let not your heart be troubled: ye believe in God, believe also in me. In my Father's house are many mansions: if it were not so, I would have told you. I go to prepare a place for you. And if I go and prepare a place for you, I will come again, and receive you unto myself; that where I am, there ye may be also" (John 14: 1-3).*

He is coming back for us someday, probably real soon. Your

Death Of A Man

soul will one day be promoted into eternity. That was God's plan all along. He wants to be with His Creation, the ones that He loves, forever. Our eternal home will be the peaceful shores of Heaven. You couldn't ask for a better ending than that! This death to self really does have a payday. It will be worth it all someday!

The Resurrection

Summary Points

- If we die (like Jesus), we will also rise again.

- We have been given a "new life" in Christ.

- We have the power of God's Spirit at work in us.

- We no longer have to be subject to our sinful nature.

- If we are tuned to His voice, we will be able to follow where He's leading.

- We can live above our circumstances.

- Heaven is our external destination, to be with Jesus throughout eternity.

Death Of A Man

Personal Reflections

(Also read Romans 8:1-39)

1. Are you dead? If you died, then you have risen again. Is Jesus living His life through you?

2. What can you do to yield to the Spirit's control in your life?

3. What things are you able to do through the Spirit that you couldn't do in your natural flesh?

4. Overcomers are victorious. What factors determine victory in the circumstances of your life?

5. How do you battle fleshly desires?

6. Do you love Jesus? Are you willing to feed His sheep? In what ways do you think you can do that?

8

The Spirit

Before His death, Jesus tried to prepare the disciples to be able to carry on long after He was gone. He told them about His death and resurrection (Mark 8:31). But He also gave them a promise, a divine promise from God, the Father, Himself. The promise was His presence, not a physical presence, but the presence of His Spirit. He promised that His Holy Spirit would be sent to them to be a comfort and a guide.

> *"Now I am going to Him who sent Me, yet none of you asks me, 'Where are you going?' Because I have said these things, you are filled with grief. But I tell you the truth: It is for your good that I am going away. Unless I go way, the Counselor (Holy Spirit) will not come to you; but if I go, I will send him to you. When he comes, he will convict the world of guilt in regard to sin and righteousness and judgment:*

> *in regard to sin, because men do not believe in Me; in regard to righteousness, because I am going to the Father, where you can see me no longer; in regard to judgment, because the prince of this world now stands condemned. I have much more to say to you, more than you can now bear. But when he, the Spirit of truth, comes he will guide you into all truth. He will not speak on his own; he will speak only what he hears, and he will tell you what is yet to come. He will bring glory to me by taking from what is mine and making it known to you"* (John 16:5-14).

The Holy Spirit has come to reveal the truth about Jesus and God's Kingdom. He will guide you into all truth if you are sensitive to His leading, as the disciples were. The disciples would go out with powerful confidence and share the "good news" about Jesus, in spite of great persecution. His Spirit would not only be with them, but would be in them. The Spirit who lead Jesus throughout His earthly ministry (Mark 1:10-12, Luke 4:1) would now be upon His followers. The Holy Spirit gives that divine power that is needed to be a strong witness for Him and carry on the mission of advancing the Kingdom of God. Jesus reassured the disciples of this just before He ascended back into Heaven.

> *"It is not for you to know the times and dates the Father has set by His own authority. But you will receive power when the Holy Spirit comes on you; and you will be my witnesses in Jerusalem, and in all Judea and Samaria, and to the ends of the earth"* (Acts 1:7, 8).

The Spirit

We, today, have the same promise available to us. God will give us power through the gift of the Holy Spirit.

However, becoming born-again and receiving the Spirit of God within you is not the end. It is just the beginning. It is the beginning of a new life. A new life that must be lived everyday in every way as His Spirit leads you. Paul said he had to die daily (I Corinthians 15:31). Everyday we must crucify our flesh and yield to the life in the Spirit that God has placed within us.

"This I say then, Walk in the Spirit, and ye shall not fulfil the lust of the flesh" (Gal. 5:16).

To live in the Spirit means we must walk in the Spirit. Learning to walk in the Spirit is much more difficult than when we first learned to walk physically. Walking in the flesh comes naturally, from pure instinct. But walking in the Spirit takes a continual yielding to the Spirit and a continual resisting of our natural instincts or desires.

It is a conscious submission and obedience to the Spirit of God that dwells within the heart of all those who believe in Jesus Christ as their Savior. God has created us with a spirit. Because of that, He is able to enter our lives through this spiritual realm. We can communicate spirit-to-spirit. His Holy Spirit has been given to you, put into your heart. We must access Him, let Him speak to us and guide us (John 16:13). Don't ignore His prodding, convictions, or inspirations. We must accommodate Him. Provide an atmosphere in your heart where He is comfortable to dwell. We do this through obedience, faithfulness, purity, and sensitivity to spiritual things. When His Spirit is in control then our flesh or self is defeated, passive, lying dormant on the battlefield of our heart. Our heart, the garden of our soul, where we make critical choices, is also a battlefield where the Spirit and the flesh contend for control. The desires of hunger, pleasure, and pride will take a back seat and will be subject unto us, if the Spirit man is allowed to reign.

> *"But I keep under my body, and bring it into subjection: lest that by any means, when I have preached to others, I myself should be a castaway" (I Cor. 9:27).*

If it is your desire to serve the Lord, you must remember this one very important spiritual truth: What you feed grows and what you starve dies.

In order to successfully walk in the Spirit, first of all you must have desire. This passionate desire must come from a sincere and humbled heart. It must be a complete and decisive act of your will. An act of our will ignites the power of the Spirit of God to begin His work in us. You must have an unquenchable determination to serve God in whatever way you can. You have to have a zeal for the Kingdom of God, to catch the vision of God's overall and specific plans. Allow the Spirit of the Lord to burden your heart with the needs of others. The needs around you, whether physical, material, intellectual, or spiritual become your responsibility as Christ's servant. Finally you must have an unwavering obedience to God, the Father, and His Word. If you don't have that desire, pray to God that He would give it to you.

> *"Delight thyself also in the Lord: and he shall give thee the desires of thine heart. Commit thy way unto the Lord; trust also in him; and he shall bring it to pass" (Psalm 37:4, 5).*

The Spirit

You may have to give up your dreams, but He will give you new and better ones.

Secondly, you must feed your spirit. As the Spirit man in you is fed, He will grow. We must have an active and positive relationship with God, the Father, His Son, and His Holy Spirit. They all play a role in guiding and encouraging us as we grow spiritually. We must pray always.

"Pray without ceasing" (I Thess. 5:17).

We must be constantly in the Word. It is the meat for our spirits and our souls. We must offer our bodies to God and renew our minds.

> ***"Therefore, I urge you, brothers, in view of God's mercy, to offer your bodies as living sacrifices, holy and pleasing to God – this is your spiritual act of worship. Do not conform any longer to the pattern of this world, but be transformed by the renewing of your mind. Then you will be able to test and approve what God's will is – His good, pleasing and perfect will" (Rom. 12:1, 2).***

How could it be any plainer than that? We must sacrifice the desires of the flesh in order to please God and do His will. We are not sacrificed to death, but we are a "living sacrifice." We sacrifice our lives daily for His kingdom. That's an act of our worship to Him. Paul states two ways that we do this. One is by not being conformed or controlled by social norms, or the patterns of this world. But be transformed or changed into something different by renewing your mind or way of thinking.

We all must reprogram our minds to think according to God's Word. Paul expounds on this in his letter to the Thessalonians.

> *"It is God's will that you should be sanctified: that you should avoid sexual immorality; that each of you should learn to control his own body in a way that is holy and honorable, not in passionate lust like the heathen, who do not know God; and that in this matter no one should wrong his brother or take advantage of him. The Lord will punish men for all such sins, as we have already told you and warned you. For God did not call us to be impure, but to live a holy life" (I Thess. 4:3- 7).*

Sexual impurity is not a part of God's Kingdom (I Cor. 6: 9, 10). The body was not made for sexual impurity. It was made for God's habitation (I Cor 6:13). We belong to God.

> *"Flee fornication. Every sin that a man doeth is without the body; but he that committeth fornication sinneth against his own body. What? know ye not that your body is the temple of the Holy Ghost which is in you, which ye have of God, and ye are not your own? For ye are bought with a price: therefore glorify God in your body, and in your spirit, which are God's" (I Cor. 6: 18-20).*

He created us. Then, He lost us because sin separated us from Him. Then, He bought us back with Jesus' blood; we are now His. We must be pure before Him. You have to deny your sexual desires. Let them be fulfilled only through your marriage partner. This takes will-power, self-discipline, and the power of the Holy Spirit. It is your sacrifice unto the Lord. This sacrifice is holy to the Lord. It is reasonable when you consider that He died to give us new life and heaven too!

The key is to not be caught up with the things of this world. The riches, prestige and allurements of this world will soon fade. But God's kingdom is eternal and He wants you to be a part of it and not a part of the kingdom of this world. But you have to transform your thinking. Think about God and His Word, the truth. Train yourself to think in spiritual terms and not in natural terms. This is a daily chore. That is why Paul used the term "renewing." It is on-going. Don't get lazy or complacent. The Devil is always awake. He is ready to pounce at any moment. Stay busy, in daily battle for good. As they say, *an idle mind is the Devil's workshop*; keep your mind on the task before you. When you make this a habit in your life, you will be able to discover God's perfect will for you. However, it does take an "attitude adjustment."

Align your thinking, attitudes, and motives with the Word of God and His Holy Spirit. Map out strategies. Prepare for battle. Put on your armor, for this is war!

> **"Finally, be strong in the Lord and in his mighty power. Put on the full armor of God, so that you can take your stand against the devil's schemes. For our struggle is not against flesh and blood, but against the rulers, against the authorities, against the powers of this dark world and against the spiritual forces of evil in the heavenly realms. Therefore put on the full armor of God, so that when the day of evil comes, you may be able to stand your ground, and after you have done everything, to stand.**

Death Of A Man

Stand firm then, with the belt of truth buckled around your waist, with the breastplate of righteousness in place, and with your feet fitted with the readiness that comes from the gospel of peace. In addition to all this, take up the shield of faith, with which you can extinguish all the flaming arrows of the evil one. Take the helmet of salvation and the sword of the Spirit, which is the word of God" (Eph. 6:10-17).

It takes spiritual weapons to fight spiritual battles. Sin is no longer in control. You are in the driver's seat. We must take this Christian life seriously. It's war, spiritual warfare. It's life or death. Some will win and some will lose. Paul tries to help us here, to win. Know your enemy. The enemy is not your brother, the church, a different denomination or political party, your neighbor, or another nation or nationality. It's the Devil. He is the one that we are really battling. It's the Devil and his army and the Lord and His army in a mass spiritual war in the heavenly realm; the realm of the unseen forces of this world. It is literally a power struggle for planet earth and its residence. We must be ready and equipped to do battle daily, so that in the end we will still be standing. Truth and righteousness are on our side. We carry that banner. The gospel is our foundation, our basic training manual. It maps out our strategies and gives us comfort and direction throughout our battle. Faith is our internal motivation. It gives us the determination to withstand any onslaught of the enemy. And finally, it is God's Spirit within us that enables and empowers us to conquer any foe, and give us victory in every battle.

We must be like our Captain, Jesus. Be conformed to His image. Let Him live His life through you. God wants to "win" through you! God wants to win the spiritual battle inside you

The Spirit

as well. He wants us to be just like His son, Jesus. He was loving, kind, caring, faithful, honest, and trustworthy (I could go on!). Yet He tells us that we can just be like Him,

> ***"Verily, verily, I say unto you, He that believeth on me, the works that I do shall he do also; and greater works than these shall he do; because I go unto my Father" (John 14:12).***

We must have faith. We must believe in the power of the Spirit. We must trust God completely. When we are fearful, we are not trusting. When we worry, we are not trusting. Faith that is genuine and active will overcome worry and fear. If you can't trust Him, you sure can't become like Him. We have heard it many times and have even sung about being like Jesus. Now it's time to put it into practice.

Finally, in order to walk in the Spirit, we must starve the flesh (so it dies!). Even though crucified, it is all too easy for the flesh to raise its ugly head and demand its own way. Like Satan, himself, the sinful flesh is always devising ways to get what it wants and seize control of our minds and bodies.

> ***"For they that are after the flesh do mind the things of the flesh; but they that are after the Spirit the things of the Spirit. For to be carnally minded is death; but to be spiritually minded is life and peace. Because the carnal mind is enmity against God: for it is not subject to the law of God, neither indeed can be. So then they that are in the flesh cannot please God" (Rom. 8:5-8).***

Don't give him an inch, don't feed him a crumb. He won't stop until he's got it all! Crucify <u>him</u> daily! Satan crucified Jesus, so let's crucify him and eliminate him from our lives. Don't listen to his lies. He will twist the truths of God around for his own benefit and your demise.

> *"Submit yourselves therefore to God. Resist the devil, and he will flee from you" (James 4:7).*

You can starve the flesh by burying pride. Pride is flesh food. Pride will butt heads with the knowledge of God and the Spirit of God. You can't have it your way and God's way. Pride has destroyed many a Christian.

> *"Pride goeth before destruction, and an haughty spirit before a fall" (Proverbs 16:18)* and *"For whosoever exalteth himself shall be abased; and he that humbleth himself shall be exalted" (Luke 14:11).*

Pride says, (not always verbally) "I'm better than they are! I deserve better than this! I'm not being treated fairly!" It is obviously very self-centered, yet some people don't see it. Pride shows itself as well through criticism and complaining. Making other people look bad, makes ourselves look better. That's pride! We are not "better" than anyone else. We are humble, but we don't have to go around and brag about it. Paul warns us to guard against arrogance.

> *"For I say, through the grace given unto me, to every man that is among you, not to think of himself more highly than he ought to think; but to think soberly, according as God hath dealt to*

The Spirit

> ***every man the measure of faith. For as we have many members in one body, and all members have not the same office: So we, being many, are one body in Christ, and every one members one of another" (Rom. 12: 3-5).***

We are one in Christ! If you want to live for God and walk in the Spirit, pride in every form must go! To starve the flesh, you must deny your fleshly desires. Your body will often cry out, "I want it!" However, you must simply say "NO!" and move on. Don't sit around and discuss or debate the issue or eventually the flesh will convince you to compromise. Say "NO!" and get yourself doing or thinking something else, immediately. Just like Joseph ran from Potipher's wife when she tempted him to commit adultery. RUN, even if it means leaving your coat behind (or your pride, or your personal gratification). If Samson would have run from Delilah when she tempted him to reveal the secret of his strength, he might have won a lot more victories for the Lord. Instead, he died along with his enemies in his final victory as he knocked down the palace pillars killing everyone inside. It's not hard, but it takes DISCIPLINE. Discipline is something that's achieved little by little, day by day. Deny, deny, I say deny those lustful desires. Natural desires are cravings to fulfill a fleshly need and generally come from our sinful nature. These are contrary to God's Word and are the stumbling blocks in our Christian walk. The best way to starve the flesh is to ignore it. Become negligent in catering to its needs. Set your mind and heart on things above.

> ***"If ye then be risen with Christ, seek those things which are above, where Christ sitteth on the right hand of God. Set your affection on things above, not on things on the earth" (Col. 3:1,2).***

Don't give it the attention that it's screaming for. Let it go to its grave, kicking and screaming all the way. The "Old Man", your flesh, does not have your best interest at heart. He will destroy your spirit and eventually your soul. Kill him! Kill him, so you can live righteously and godly.

> *"For the grace of God has appeared that offers salvation to all people. It teaches us to say "No" to ungodliness and worldly passions, and to live self-controlled, upright and godly lives in this present age" (Titus 2:11-13).*

Trust in the grace of God. He is faithful and will help you in your times of temptation.

> *"There hath no temptation taken you but such as is common to man: but God is faithful, who will not suffer you to be tempted above that ye are able; but will with the temptation also make a way to escape, that ye may be able to bear it" (I Cor. 10: 13).*

It may be tough, but you can do it; you must do it. God's Spirit in us must defeat our flesh and sinful nature. It's a matter of life and death. Either your flesh dies or your spirit dies. The choice is yours!

Once you have overcome through the power of God by feeding the spirit and starving the flesh, then you are in a position to serve. Serving the Lord brings the greatest joy in all the world. We serve by first following our example. Jesus became a humbled servant (Philippians 2:5-8). Are you willing to do the same? Another way we serve the Lord is by being an example to others.

> *"Don't let anyone look down on you because you are young, but set an example for the believers in speech, in conduct, in love, in faith and in purity" (I Tim. 4:12).*

Show your family, friends, co-workers, and fellow Christians what a real Christian is like. Be a servant of love and compassion, seeking to be a blessing to all you come in contact with. And finally, give! Give of yourself to others. We serve God by serving others. Jesus encouraged us to serve the less fortunate.

> *"In as much as you have done it for the least of these my brethren, you have done in unto Me" (Matt. 25:40).*

Give whatever you have and whatever you are to God, so He can use it to advance the Kingdom of God in the lives of others. Peter gave what he had to the crippled man.

> *"Silver and gold, I don't have, but what I do have, I give to you, in the name of Jesus of Nazareth, walk!" (Acts 3:6).*

The power in the name of Jesus can heal the sick. His power is available to all His followers. We've got a lot when we have the power of God working through us. Give whatever you have, nothing is insignificant to God. Little is much when placed in the hands of God. Nothing is too difficult for God.

"Jesus said unto him, If thou canst believe, all things are possible to him that believeth" (Mark 9:23).

Living your life controlled by the Spirit of God will be your greatest challenge. It is the greatest opportunity that God affords you and it will provide your greatest satisfaction. It takes a day-by-day commitment. It's a great journey when we do it God's way. The end is in sight.

The Spirit

Summary Points

- You must have a desire to live according to the leading of the very Spirit of God, who is within you.

- If we live according to the desires of our flesh we will die but if we live according to the Spirit, we will live.

- It is God's will for you to avoid sexual immorality.

- The key to living in the Spirit is to not get caught up with the things of this world. We must resist the Devil and say no to pride and sin.

- What you feed, grows. What you starve, dies.

- The by-product of living in the Spirit is a longing and willingness to give, love, and serve others.

Death Of A Man

Personal Reflections
(Also read Romans 7:7-25)

1. Which area of the fleshly desires is your most difficult struggle?

2. In what circumstances did you find yourself when it was most difficult to resist the temptation?

3. What things have you done in the past that has helped you to overcome this temptation?

4. What things can you do ahead of time to be prepared for the upcoming temptations?

5. What encouraging scriptures speak direct truth to this situation?

6. What steps can you take to live a life controlled by the Spirit of God?

9

The Ascension

Jesus returned to the place where it all started, the Garden of Gethsemane. Then He went a little further, this time in the opposite direction and to a different mount. He had finished His life work on Mount Calvary and now He was about to complete His earthly ministry on the Mount of Olives. Jesus could remember just a few years back when He preached His most notable sermon, "The Sermon on the Mount." How it must have seemed like only yesterday. From there He was able to look across the Kidron Valley to the Holy City, Jerusalem. He could remember all the sacrifices that He had made for the people He deeply loved (including you and I). What a feeling of accomplishment He must have had that day. He knew that He had fulfilled all that the Father had sent Him to do. Will you be able to experience that same feeling? If you keep following Jesus you will. Then with one last prayer for His disciples, He left them with a final blessing. Then…He was gone! He ascended up into the clouds to be seated in the Heavenlies at the right hand of God, the Father. Jesus went back to Heaven. He came and did what He had to do and when He was done, He went back home.

> *"After He said this, He was taken up before their eyes, and a cloud hid Him from their sight. They were looking intently up into the sky as He was going, when suddenly two men dressed in white stood beside them. 'Men of Galilee,' they said, 'why do you stand here looking into the sky? This same Jesus, who has been taken from you into heaven will come back in the same way you have seen Him go into heaven"* (Acts 1:9-11).

Actually, He is not quite done, He will be back, but He did finish the work that He came to do. He won the victory over death, hell, and the grave. Jesus won!

He won for you: so, you have won! You are victorious. Now we need to live in victory every day. If you have followed Jesus all the way, then you are dead to sin and your selfish way of life and have risen to a new life of righteousness to serve the living God. Jesus died for you and now you have died for Him. You have been set free from the bondage of sin, lust, and pride. Paul writes in Colossians 2:14 that the sentence you deserved for your sin has been satisfied. The "writ of ordinances" used to be put over a prisoners cell door which stated his punishable crime. When his sentence was served completely they would blot out the handwriting of that ordinance. They would write over the top of it, "It is finished." The sentence had been served and penalty paid in full. When Jesus said from the cross, "It is finished," the price of our sins had been paid, the punishment satisfied! Our sins have been blotted out, forgiven, and

The Ascension

forgotten. We are free! Jesus paid it all. The chains of bondage have been loosed and the prison doors have swung open wide.

It is sad to say that many Christians have become so comfortable in their "old lives," (their prison cells) that they never taste real freedom. When Jesus died, He descended into Satan's domain (the earth) to take away the keys to death and the grave. With resurrection power, He has freed us from Satan's grip and the power of sin over us. Our freedom and power over sin depends upon Jesus' sacrificial death, not on our works. But, it also depends upon our death. Yes, we too must die. Sometimes death sounds so horrible, so final. Someone once wrote, "Born once, die twice, born twice, die once." You must be born again! Another way to say it is, die once, dead forever; die twice live forever. Jesus knew and taught that death brings life for those who receive Him as Lord. It's not an end, it is a transition. The same is true of physical death for the believer.

> *"But I would not have you to be ignorant, brethren, concerning them which are asleep, that ye sorrow not, even as others which have no hope. For if we believe that Jesus died and rose again, even so them also which sleep in Jesus will God bring with him. For this we say unto you by the word of the Lord, that we which are alive and remain unto the coming of the Lord shall not prevent them which are asleep. For the Lord himself shall descend from heaven with a shout, with the voice of the archangel, and with the trump of God: and the dead in Christ shall rise first: Then we which are alive and remain shall be caught up together with them in the clouds, to meet the Lord in the air: and so shall*

we ever be with the Lord. Wherefore comfort one another with these words" (I Thess. 4:13-18).

Heaven awaits the Christian when he or she dies. Jesus is coming again! He is coming back for His people, His followers, those who have died to self and who live for Him.

How do you die? You can talk about crucifying the flesh. You can hear about it over and over again, but if you don't have any practical methods or any ideas of how to deal with the flesh, you'll be frustrated and hopeless. You hear, "starve the flesh, so it will die." But what does that really mean? Here are some other helpful hints that will serve as ammunition in defeating the "old man," the flesh. Jesus sacrificed His body for us and now our bodies are to be a sacrifice to Him. We must crucify the flesh so that we can live for and serve God. There is one way to crucify the flesh that I learned when I was just a child. It came to me by way of a little song that we used to sing. It went like this:

> *"O be careful little hands what you do. O be careful little hands what you do. For the Father up above is looking down in love, so be careful little hands what you do."*

Of course we had motions to the song to reinforce the meaning of the words. And if you know the song, then you know that there are at least four other verses.

> *"O be careful little feet where you go,"*
> *"O be careful little ears what you hear,"*
> *"O be careful little eyes what you see,"*
> *"O be careful little mouth what you say."*

The Ascension

The key to living the Christian life, living victoriously, serving God, and crucifying the flesh could all be summed up in this little song. However, I would add; "O be careful little mind what you think." What we do with our bodies has a profound and direct effect on our spiritual lives. We are in control of our bodies. We have been given a free will to choose and decide what we do with our bodies. We choose what we look at, hear, touch, say, and where we go. If our bodies are under God's control, then we will do the things that please Him.

The eyes are so important in our battle over the flesh. The eyes are the windows to the mind. Our eyes see a lot of things, but we choose to single out certain things to focus on. We must train and condition ourselves not to focus in on those things that are pleasing to the flesh. If you buy a new car, you suddenly see that same car all over town. You had never noticed so many of them before but now your mind was conditioned, or re-programmed to see them. Many times we see what we want to see, or what we have been re-programmed to look at. God labeled three main areas of sin; the lust of the eyes, the lust of the flesh, and the pride of life (I John 2:16). He realizes that the eyes can be used in many ways to cause someone to sin. Jesus spoke of the eyes in that great "Sermon on the Mount."

> ***"But I say unto you, That whosoever looketh on a woman to lust after her hath committed adultery with her already in his heart. And if thy right eye offend thee, pluck it out, and cast it from thee: for it is profitable for thee that one of thy members should perish, and not that thy whole body should be cast into hell" (Matt. 5:28,29).***

The temptation to lust is very strong in western culture today. We are bombarded with inappropriate images all the time. It's not even necessary to list all the sources that the Devil uses to entice us to fuel our lust by watching or observing these lustful temptations. Simply put, it is vital, and I mean vital, that we guard our eyes and avoid these images that could be plastered to the walls of our minds.

As the scripture says, your eyes could cause you to sin and end up in Hell. It's critical that we maintain our focus. Paul tells us where our focus should be.

> *"Looking unto Jesus, the author and finisher of our faith" (Heb. 12:2).*

That's our focus, Him, the one who loved us and gave Himself for us.

> *"Brethren, I count not myself to have apprehended: but this one thing I do, forgetting those things which are behind, and reaching forth unto those things which are before, I press toward the mark for the prize of the high calling of God in Christ Jesus" (Phil. 3:13, 14).*

Paul's focus was on the prize, the Kingdom of God and eternal life. Our goal each day is to remain on the path that leads us home, to our eternal home.

Job, of the Old Testament, realized the virtue of keeping your eyes where they belong and not on things that would cause you to sin.

> *"I made a covenant with my eyes not to look lustfully at a girl. For what is man's lot from*

The Ascension

God above, his heritage from the Almighty on high? Is it not ruin for the wicked, disaster for those who do wrong? Does He not see my ways and count my every step?" (Job 31:1– 4).

We must covenant with God to not look lustfully at another person. We must subject our bodies to that commitment of purity. Man was made for a much higher purpose than for him to just seek the pleasure of his flesh and fulfillment of his human desires. Disaster will come upon the one who cannot discipline themselves in the area. The pornography business is at an all-time high. Many are falling prey to these lustful temptations and traps. You must guard what your eyes see. God is always watching!

Our ears are no different. What we choose to listen to can also cause us to sin and end up in Hell. What we listen to will have a significant effect on our behavior. It has been proven through the years that audible suggestions repeated enough times will solicit a specified behavior. Certain words, music, and even tones can change someone's attitude, outlook, and even their health. The old saying, "Garbage in, Garbage out," reflects the truth that what you take in audibly will come back verbally. What goes in through the auditory nerve, goes directly to the brain, and can be retrieved either consciously or subconsciously. Haven't you caught yourself singing a little jingle or a line to a song before you even realized what you just said? Things come out of our mouths involuntarily at times. But only what has gone in can come out.

Jesus' own words in the book of Luke confirm this to be true.

"The good man brings good things out of the good stored up in his heart, and the evil man

brings evil things out of the evil stored up in his heart. For out of the overflow of his heart his mouth speaks" (Luke 6: 45).

    Good men do good things when there is good in their hearts. What is stored up in the container of your heart? The answer is whatever you have allowed to come in from the outside. We can't filter what we hear and just keep what we want and dispose of everything else. Once it's in there, it's in there and could very easily come out and sometimes involuntarily or at the wrong time. We can guard what comes in by being proactive. Don't put yourself in situations where you know that you will hear things that are not pleasing to God. You can avoid the person who tells the inappropriate jokes or who has a foul mouth. You can choose the kind of music and television shows that send messages through the ears to your brain. In our culture today, sometimes we will simply have to learn to tune some things out in order to live a life of purity.

    It would be very difficult to stay on the path of righteousness when we continue to feed our mind messages that are contrary to God's Will and His Word, in other words, "the way of the world."

    And speaking about the words we speak, they are powerful.

"Death and life are in the power of the tongue" (Prov. 18:21).

Even though James tells us that it is an unruly member of our body, with God's help we can guard our mouths and control our tongues. James gives us a hint on how to do it. He tells us to be quick to listen, slow to speak (James 1:19). As many a mom and teacher have said, "Think before you speak." Those words are words that all of us need to hear over and over again. The Bible

The Ascension

encourages us to speak life and blessing to one another. It tells us to speak words of encouragement.

> *"Let no corrupt communication proceed out of your mouth, but that which is good to the use of edifying, that it may minister grace unto the hearers"(Eph. 4:29).*

Don't have a filthy mouth or even use words in bad taste. Don't try to be the "life of the party" by telling off-colored jokes.

> *"Nor should there be obscenity, foolish talk, or coarse joking, which are out of place, but rather thanksgiving" (Eph. 5:4).*

Be encouraging and build up one another. A kind word goes a long way. Don't tear one another down. Don't criticize, complain, or argue.

> *"Do everything without complaining or arguing, so that you may become blameless and pure, children of God without fault in a crooked and depraved generation, in which you shine like stars in the universe" (Phil. 2:14, 15).*

If you are encouraging and positive, you will stand out in this world. Your light will shine bright and lighten up the world around you wherever you go. Like Paul told Timothy, be an example to others in your speech (I Timothy 4:12). A well known preacher once said that he would pray a certain scripture every morning before he started his day. I liked it, so I decided to try to pray it myself every morning.

"May the words of my mouth and the meditation of my heart be pleasing in Your sight, O Lord, my Rock, and my Redeemer" (Psalm 19:14).

Let your words speak life and hope. Let them reflect the love of God that is within you. Tell others about the truth of God's Word and His love for them. You are God's mouthpiece. You are His ambassador. Speak His words. If you want to see good days, then follow Peter's instruction.

"For whoever would love life and see good days must keep his tongue from evil and his lips from deceitful speech" (I Peter 3:10).

You will judged by your words (Matt. 12: 36, 37).

Your hands and your feet are not as difficult to control. Usually it takes a premeditated thought before we put them into action. There are things that we shouldn't touch and there are places we shouldn't go. These things may differ slightly from person to person, but the true Christian is sensitive to the indwelling Holy Spirit and His conviction about such things. And Paul tells us in Colossians 3:17 to do everything in the name of Jesus, with thankfulness to God.

"How beautiful are the feet of him that brings good news" (Rom. 10:15).

Let your hands and feet serve the Lord your God, wherever you go and whatever you do.

"Make it your ambition to lead a quiet life, to mind your own business and to work with your

The Ascension

> *hands, just as we told you, so that your daily life may win the respect of outsiders and so that you will not be dependent on anybody" (I Thess. 4:11, 12).*

We are instructed in God's word that our hands are for work. Use them as God has given you special ability. Your hands are also used in prayer and worship. We lay our hands on people when we pray for them as a point of contact as an expression of compassion and concern. Our touch unites us in faith with the other person. Our hands are used in worship as we lift holy hands unto the Lord. (Psalm 63:4) If we use our feet to serve God then we will go where he leads. We cannot fulfill the Lord's great commission unless we use our feet and "go."

> *"Go into all the world and preach the good news to all creation" (Mark 16:15).*

Finally, let us consider my added verse about the mind. What we choose to think about has a definite and direct affect on our behavior. Phillippians 4:8 tells us to think about good things that are proper, pure, and uplifting to the Lord and others. Mind control must be practiced.

> *"The weapons we fight with are not the weapons of the world. On the contrary, they have divine power to demolish strongholds. We demolish arguments and every pretension that sets itself up against the knowledge of God, and we take captive every thought to make it obedient to Christ" (II Cor. 10:4, 5).*

We must take control of every thought that comes into our minds. God has given us the power to do that. The enemy will usually try to lie and deceive with very convincing arguments. However, when it does not measure up to the truth, we must stand on God's Word and remain obedient to it. Read the Bible, study the Bible, memorize the Bible, and meditate on His Word.

It won't happen overnight, but as you fill your mind each day with the things of God and the Word of God, you will be conditioned to think like Jesus. We are reminded several times in His Word to take on the "mind of Christ." The "W.W.J.D. generation," asked, "What would Jesus do?" so as to live their lives following Jesus' example. Well, what would Jesus think? From what is recorded in scripture, it seems that Jesus was always thinking about others. He was not self-absorbed, self-centered, or selfish, He was constantly doing for other people. He was constantly seeking to please God, the Father. That's what taking up your cross is all about, living your life following Jesus' example.

The slogan says, "attitude is everything." You have to set your heart and mind to the task with an unwavering determination. You must intentionally and with premeditation, deny yourself, pick up your cross, and follow JESUS! Now that you are experiencing a new life from God, a life of victory, what kind of life can you expect to enjoy? Let's take a look.

The Ascension

Summary Points

- We have been set free from the prison of the sinful nature. Live in liberty.

- Death is not an end, it is a transition. You have been given "new" life.

- Guard what you see and what you hear, it can make or break you.

- Let your words be pleasing to God and others. Think before you speak.

- Offer your body as a living and holy sacrifice to God. Be pure by saying "no" to lust.

- Win the battle of the mind with the spiritual weapons from God. Think in terms of godly, not worldly.

Death Of A Man

Personal Reflections

(Also read II Timothy 2: 14-26)

1. What are some specific things that God has spoken to you about not seeing or looking at?

2. What are some things that you feel should not go in through your auditory system? How can you keep this from happening?

3. What has helped you from saying things that you know shouldn't be said?

4. What things can we put into practice that would help us to be a better encourager?

5. How does God help us from getting our hand in the "cookie jar?"

6. What can you implement into your life today to help condition your mind toward the things of God?

10
The Life

Why? Why would someone choose to go through all this: dying to self and worldly pleasures; sacrificing one's own rights, desires, and dreams; putting others first; and yielding control of their lives to someone else? Well, you wouldn't trade your "life" in for something that was not better. With Jesus on the throne of your heart and His Spirit guiding your every step, you will experience a life far better that you could ever expect or imagine.

"Now to Him who is able to do immeasurably more than all we ask or imagine, according to His power that is at work within us" (Eph. 3:20).

But, the only way to experience this kind of life is by *"The Death of a Man."* When you die to the life you are trying to make for yourself, then God can give you the life that He has planned for you. When we follow Jesus completely, we not only become like Him, we actually become one with Him. That is exactly what Jesus prayed for when He prayed to God, the Father, in John chapter 17.

> *"My prayer is not for them alone. I pray also for those who will believe in me through their message, that all of them may be one, Father, just as you are in me and I am in you. May they also be in us so that the world may believe that you have sent me. I have given them the glory that you gave me, that they may be one as we are one, I in them and you in me, so that they may be brought to complete unity. Then the world will know that you sent me and have loved them even as you have loved me. Father, I want those you have given me to be with me where I am, and to see my glory, the glory you have given me because you loved me before the creation of the world. Righteous Father, though the world does not know you, I know you, and they know that you have sent me. I have made you known to them, and will continue to make you known in order that the love you have for me may be in them and that I myself may be in them" (John 17:20-26).*

We are one with Jesus and His love is in us. That's a great foundation for a great life. That's the kind of life this death of a man brings? Jesus calls it abundant life (John 10:10). It is eternal, never-ending, and one day, we will have a glorified body, just like Jesus! This life is a new life in a new realm or a new kingdom. The Bible refers to it as the Kingdom of God. Paul describes God's kingdom for us.

> *"For the Kingdom of God is not a matter of*

The Life

> *eating and drinking, (not a physical kingdom) but of righteousness, peace, and joy in the Holy Spirit" (Rom. 14:17).*

Although He is in control, Jesus does not rule this world, at present.

> *"Jesus answered, My kingdom is not of this world: if my kingdom were of this world, then would my servants fight, that I should not be delivered to the Jews: but now is my kingdom not from hence" (John 18:36).*

We must realize this as well. Our kingdom is not of this world. We belong to another world; we belong to God. We must not live for the things of this world.

> *"Love not the world, neither the things that are in the world. If any man love the world, the love of the Father is not in him. For all that is in the world, the lust of the flesh, and the lust of the eyes, and the pride of life, is not of the Father, but is of the world. And the world passeth away, and the lust thereof: but he that doeth the will of God abideth for ever" (I John 2: 15-17).*

God's kingdom is a spiritual kingdom. However, it is not one that floats somewhere in outer space. The kingdom of God is within us. We are made up of body, soul, and spirit. God's kingdom can be found within the spirit of man, as he opens his spirit up to the Spirit of God. We are able to have a daily relationship with God, spirit to spirit. Success in the spiritual realm (the Kingdom of God) is not dependent upon material things. The Bible refers to these things as "earthly" or "worldly." When we experience "*The Death of a Man,*" dying to our sinful (natural) nature, we are born-again of the spirit. Jesus explained this to a Jewish ruler named Nicodemus one night.

> ***"Jesus answered, Verily, verily, I say unto thee, Except a man be born of water and of the Spirit, he cannot enter into the kingdom of God. That which is born of the flesh is flesh; and that which is born of the Spirit is spirit. Marvel not that I said unto thee, Ye must be born again. The wind bloweth where it listeth, and thou hearest the sound thereof, but canst not tell whence it cometh, and whither it goeth: so is every one that is born of the Spirit" (John 3:5-8).***

As we spend time in prayer and reading the Bible our spirit begins to grow in an understanding of who God is and who we are ourselves. "*The Death of a Man*" is not a one-time event like Jesus' death was. It is a daily, progressive, on-going process. It is a conscious decision that must be made not just each and every day, but each and every hour, minute, and second. We must purposely walk in this new life that we have been given (Romans 6:4). As we walk in this new "Kingdom of God," we will experience that righteousness, peace, and joy. Along with that comes a complete fulfillment of your divine purpose and a self-fulfillment that cannot be experienced any other way. God puts within you His Righteousness which enables you to do what is "right" in His sight. It empowers you to act in a similar manner to God Himself in your relationship to others. That power is the Holy Spirit. When Jesus came into your heart, He planted the seed of the Spirit, His Spirit. When you feed and nurture that seed, it will produce a crop. You will be able to love unconditionally. You will be able to forgive those who have hurt you. You will be able to resist the temptations of the Devil and the world around you as you experience the Kingdom of God in your life. In Acts 1:8 Paul verifies that this power comes to us in the form of God's Holy Spirit. Jesus said that the Father would not withhold the Holy Spirit from him that asks (Luke 11:13). The fruit that is produced or the evidence of God's Spirit is listed by Paul.

> *"But the fruit of the Spirit is love, joy, peace, patience, kindness, goodness, faithfulness, gentleness, and self-control (Gal. 5:22).*

These are the things that are exhibited in the life of a person who is dead to sin and alive to righteousness, serving the Lord. The previous verses listed the things that are found in the life of a person who is not dead to sin.

> *"The acts of the sinful nature are obvious: sexual immorality, impurity and debauchery, idolatry and witchcraft; hatred, discord, jealousy, fits of rage, selfish ambition, dissensions, factions and envy, drunkenness, orgies, and the like. I warn you as I did before, that those who live like this will not inherit the kingdom of God" (Gal. 5:19 - 21).*

These are the words of Paul written under divine inspiration directly from the Holy Spirit of God.

According to this scripture a huge portion of our society are not going to heaven. This list just seems to accurately identify this present culture. However, it should not describe a true child of God. That's why we need to separate ourselves from the things of this world, and worldly people who live to fulfill the desires of their sinful nature.

> *"Be ye not unequally yoked together with unbelievers: for what fellowship hath righteousness with unrighteousness? and what communion hath light with darkness? And what concord hath Christ with Belial? or what part hath he that believeth with an infidel? And what agreement hath the temple of God with idols? for ye are the temple of the living God; as God hath said, I will dwell in them, and walk in them; and I will be their God, and they shall be my people. Wherefore come out from among them, and be ye separate, saith the Lord, and touch not the unclean thing; and I will receive you. And will be a Father unto you, and ye shall be my sons and daughters, saith the Lord Almighty" (II Cor. 6:14-18).*

We are different! We are the temple of the living God. We need to allow His Spirit to control our lives and let the fruit of God's Spirit characterize our lives. It is God who provides the love that all of us crave. We were born with a capacity to receive love and a propensity to give it. Without God there is no love.

> *"Dear friends, let us love one another, for love comes from God. Everyone who loves has been born of God and knows God. Whoever does not love does not know God, because God is love (I John 4:7, 8).*

The Life

We must love as Jesus loved. He loved everyone, everywhere, all the time. True, He had to rebuke some people once in a while, but He still loved them. Not only did Jesus love, but He also served. It goes hand-in-hand. Jesus instructed us that if we would to be great in His kingdom, then we must be a servant.

> *"Instead, whoever wants to become great among you must be your servant" (Matt. 20:27).*

Jesus again explained it in the book of Luke. While Jesus met with His disciples at that "Last Supper", He reminded them that His Kingdom is not like the kingdoms of this world.

> *"Instead, the greatest among you should be like the youngest, and the one who rules like the one who serves. For who is greater, the one who is at the table or the one who serves? Is it not the one who is at the table? But I am among you as one who serves" (Luke 22:26, 27).*

We are not better than Jesus. He is the one we are serving and following. We are now accountable to follow His example. We are accountable to God and to one another. We are accountable to the scriptures, God's Word. Strive to prove yourself as a man or woman of God.

> *Do your best to present yourself to God as one approved, a workman who does not need to be ashamed and who correctly handles the word of truth" (II Tim. 2:15).*

Paul goes on to give Timothy further instruction just a few

verses later. Jesus would want us today to correctly apply these truths to our own lives.

> *"Flee the evil desires of youth, and pursue righteousness, faith, love, and peace, along with those who call on the Lord out of a pure heart. Don't have anything to do with foolish and stupid arguments, because you know they produce quarrels. And the Lord's servant must not quarrel; instead, he must be kind to everyone, able to teach, not resentful. Those who oppose him he must gently instruct, in the hope that God will grant them repentance leading them to a knowledge of the truth, and that they will come to their senses and escape from the trap of the devil, who has taken them captive to do his will" (II Tim. 2:22-26).*

Don't be selfish, self-serving, argumentative, or resentful. But rather be kind and compassionate towards others, trying to help them to come to an understanding of the truth of God. Until they do, they will continue in their bondage to sin and Satan. Lead them into the kingdom of light, hope, and freedom, the Kingdom of God. In God's kingdom, you will also have a peace that is beyond comprehension (Philippians 4:7). There is nothing more valuable in the world we live in today than peace. We cry out for it, and we long for it deep within our souls. Real peace can only come from God; it is a part of His Kingdom. Even in the midst of trials, difficulties, pain, and sorrow, His peace remains constant. It will carry us emotionally through each and every circumstance of life. His peace is the calm in every storm. Jesus told His disciples that His peace will take away their fears (John 14:27). Paul went a step further to encourage Christians to allow this peace to rule in their hearts (Colossians 3:15).

God also includes joy in this kingdom. Christians should be the happiest people in the world. We have real joy, straight from God. There's nothing like it.

> ***"I have told you this so that My joy may be in you and that your joy may be complete" (John 15:11).***

Complete joy will make you completely happy. It's a joy to know God. It's a joy to love God. It's a joy to serve God.

> ***"You have made known to me the path of life; you fill me with joy in your presence, with eternal pleasures at your right hand" (Psalm 16:11).***

Our only hope for joy comes from the God of hope, as we trust Him. This comes from the Holy Spirit (Romans 15:13). The life of a Christian should consistently show forth patience, kindness, goodness, and gentleness. We will show our care and concern for others, all others. John 13:35 says that we will be recognized as God's children when we show love to one another. We will live a life of faithfulness to God and a consistent godly life-style before the world. Finally, if we are a born-again child of God then we will show that the spirit dwelling within us enables us to exhibit self-control. We should never be "out of control." God's Spirit is in control of our lives. Remember, we are dead.

> ***"But ye are not in the flesh, but in the Spirit, if so be that the Spirit of God dwell in you. Now if any man have not the Spirit of Christ, he is***

none of his. And if Christ be in you, the body is dead because of sin; but the Spirit is life because of righteousness"(Rom. 8:9,10).

However, this decision each day is not an easy one. It is a battle. Paul speaks of the war waging in his soul in Romans 7:23. Then in Romans chapter 8 he tells us that we are more than conquerors through Jesus Christ, our Lord. If He is our Lord, then He is Master of everything. We become His servants, it is Him we should obey. We serve Him with unfeigned loyalty. And He gives us the victory again and again. Who wouldn't want this kind of life? You must be willing to give up everything. And why not? Jesus died for us! He gave us a new life! He promised us a home in heaven! He wants to give us beauty for ashes (Isaiah 61:3). He has promised us a wonderful life and a specific plan for us individually. We have nothing (of value) to lose. In fact, Jesus said that if we don't die to self and carry our cross we will lose everything. This scripture is worth repeating.

"Anyone who does not take his cross and follow me is not worthy of me. Whoever finds his life will lose it, and whoever loses his life for my sake will find it" (Matthew 10:38, 39).

Jesus tells us plainly that if you choose to hold onto this world and its pleasures, then in the end, you will lose it all. You will face judgment for rejecting Him and you will suffer eternal damnation in Hell. But if you will follow Him, carrying your cross and forsaking the pleasures of this world, then you will find a new life, an eternal one. You will experience, one day, the eternal riches of God's grace in Heaven, forever. He is coming back soon to establish His eternal kingdom.

"And, behold, I come quickly; and my reward is with me, to give every man according as his work shall be" (Rev. 22:12).

Will you be ready for Him when He comes? Are you ready today? You must first make that decision to follow Jesus, receiving Him as your personal Savior and Lord. Then you must trace His steps from the garden to the grave. Deny your fleshly, selfish desires and carry the burden of living a righteous life under God's control. Let God have His way in your life and you will find that *"The Death of a Man"* is the only way to a new life! It will be one of peace, joy, and complete fulfillment. Enjoy the journey!

The Life

Summary Points

- The Kingdom of God is within us. We commune with God, spirit to spirit.

- We must allow the Spirit of God to be in control and help us keep our bodies under control.

- God's Spirit at work in us enables us to live a godly life.

- We must separate ourselves from worldly things and worldly people.

- The fruits of God's Spirit should be evidenced in your life daily.

- If we try to make a life for ourselves, we will lose. If we give up on this life, we will win, life forever.

Personal Reflections

(Also read I Thessalonians 5:1-24)

1. What are some fruits of the Spirit that are established in your life? Which ones are hard to find?

2. What is your level of joy? Why?

3. Are there some acts of the sinful nature that are still a part of your life? What can you do about that?

4. What are some things of the flesh that seem to want to battle with your mind every day?

5. What are some new ways that you can show God's love to others?

6. Who do you know that needs to read this book? Give it to them!

11

Conclusion

I leave with you these words straight from the Bible and straight from my heart.

> *For the sake of the body, which is the church, I have become its servant by the commission God gave me to present to YOU the Word of God in its fullness - the mystery that has been kept hidden for ages and generations, but is now disclosed to the saints. To them God has chosen to make known among the Gentiles (all people groups), the glorious riches of this mystery, which is CHRIST IN YOU, the Hope of Glory"* (Col. 1:24-27).

Death Of A Man

I have felt compelled by God for over 25 years to share this message with the world. It is simply: Jesus Christ living in you is your only hope of a blessed life and that throughout eternity. Paul gave us the key and the foundation for this book.

"I am crucified with Christ, nevertheless I live, yet not I, but Christ lives in me" (Gal. 2:20).

If and when and only when, we die to our very selfish and worldly life, can God through His Son, Jesus Christ enter our lives by His indwelling Holy Spirit. We must let Jesus live His life through us, His faithful followers. We are called to be His witnesses and let His Light shine into the darkness around us. We must be Jesus to the world. It's time! So now that you have followed Jesus all the way: from the **garden** of decision; through the **valley** of self-denial; enduring the **judgment** and criticism of others; down the **road** of ridicule; carrying the **cross** of humility, servanthood, and submission; **dying** to self-will; **rising** in a new life of righteousness; and living a holy life lead by the **Spirit** of God, then there is just one thing left to do. "There's more?" you might ask. Yes, what you must do now is start all over and do it again. That's right, every day we must start anew the process of following Jesus. We have the same decision that faces us when our feet touch the ground each morning. Just because we followed Jesus yesterday, does not mean that we don't have to make that same choice today. As we have seen emphasized in God's word, we must "daily" carry our cross and "daily" be crucified with Christ (Luke 9:23 and I Cor. 15:31). We serve a living God and we are His daily living sacrifices (Rom.12:1). Our pay-off is a life of genuine love, real joy, and lasting peace. And, by the way, we also get eternal life in Heaven with Jesus. Your choice, every day! It may take days, weeks, months, or years to go through this process the first time. I hope and pray that you'll take the short-cut, unlike the Israelites, and take a few

Conclusion

days not 40 years to get to your promise land. God has promised you a glorious life if you will follow His Son, Jesus. After you have learned to be completely surrendered to God, the Father, Jesus, the Son, and the Holy Spirit then it will be easier to know how to do that every day. Here's something that might help you with this daily process. This book can be summarized in this 7-step prayer of renewed commitment to God. Pray a prayer like this every morning:

1. Lord, I surrender my own will and submit to Your will and Your plans for my life.

2. Help me to deny fleshly desires and say, "no" to every temptation.

3. Allow me to show Your love to others, even those who oppose You.

4. I bury my pride and selfishness so I can live the godly life that You have given me.

5. It's my desire to be sensitive to the leading of Your Spirit in my life, and be obedient.

6. May I, today, be a blessing to others by sharing Your love and Your truth with them.

7. I will live today in the light of eternity and in the hope of seeing You someday soon.

Get started on the right foot every day and enjoy the journey of a lifetime! You won't *ever* regret it. Thank and praise God everyday for His goodness, His mercy, and the blessings that He has given to you. And someday we will all join in one mighty chorus to sing His praise forevermore. Remember it is a walk of faith, faith that comes from God. Trust Him and He will lead you every step of the way!

If you have any questions or comments, I would love to hear from you.

Please send all correspondence to tedt101@yahoo.com.